EMBRACING AUTISM IN PRESCHOOL

SUCCESSFUL STRATEGIES FOR GENERAL EDUCATION TEACHERS

Embracing Autism in Preschool

Successful Strategies for General Education Teachers

Updated Second Edition

Karen Griffin Roberts, M.Ed.

Fourth Lloyd Productions, LLC
Burgess, VA

©2020, 2010 by Karen Griffin Roberts
All Rights Reserved

For permission to reproduce selections of this book
please contact:
Fourth Lloyd Productions, LLC
512 Old Glebe Point Road
Burgess, VA 22432
e-mail: stodart@kaballero.com
www.fourthlloydproductions.com

Printed in the USA
ISBN 978-1-7350341-1-9 paperback
Library of Congress Control Number: 2020938453

Book and cover design by Richard Stodart
Family and preschool children photos by Karen G. Roberts

To my son, Kevin David, who is my inspiration and has taught me everything I *really need to know*...

MY AUTISM

I have autism.
I have two sides,
And things are sometimes cloudy.
But, I'm like a little seed that
Grows into a flower.
I have courage,
And I am supported by family, faith and friends
Who make me feel the warmth
In my heart.

— Kevin David Roberts

BOOKS BY THE AUTHOR

LET'S TALK SERIES

Let's Talk About Autism in Early Childhood
Karen Griffin Roberts, M.Ed.

Let's Talk About Early Language Development
Ana Gamarra Hoover, M.Ed. and Karen Griffin Roberts, M.Ed.

Let's Talk About Early Childhood Social-Emotional Development
Karen Griffin Roberts, M.Ed. and Ana Gamarra Hoover, M.Ed.

Embracing Autism in Preschool, Updated Second Edition
Karen Griffin Roberts, M.Ed.

Table of Contents

Foreword xi
Preface xiii
Acknowledgements xv
Introduction xvii

Chapter One: What is Autism? 19

Autism Defined   19
The Autism "Spectrum"   22
High or Low Functioning Autism   23
Dual Diagnosis in Autism   24
How Prevalent Is Autism?   24
Learn More About Autism   25

Chapter Two: Why Inclusion? 27

Inclusion Is the Law   27
Inclusion Is Developmentally Appropriate   27
Inclusion Is the Best Practice   28
The Exemplary Preschool Classroom   28

Chapter Three: Language and Communication 31

Language and Communication in Preschoolers   31
Language and Communication in Autism   32
    Pragmatic Language Delay   32
    Theory of Mind   32
    Functional Communication   32
    Receptive and Expressive Language   33
    Reciprocal Communication   33

Example of a Child with Autism/Communication Deficits   33
Classroom Strategies to Assist Development of Language and Communication   36
Provide Visual Support   36
    Visual Schedules   36
    Picture Exchange Communication Systems (PECS)   36
Enhancing Verbal Instruction   38
Provide Instruction for All Learning Styles   38
Be Certain All Children Are Attentive and Engaged   38
Playing Games   39
Use Music to Communicate   39
READ! READ! READ!   40
Manipulatives, Puppets and Humor   40
Important Considerations for Communicating With Children   40

Chapter Four: Social Skills in Autism   43

Social Skills for Preschoolers   43
    Social Reciprocity   43
    Joint Attention and Social Sharing   44
    Reading Social Cues   44
    Example of a Child With Autism and Social Skills Deficits   45
Classroom Strategies To Assist Social Skills Development   47
    Social Narratives and Picture Books in the Mainstream   47
    Social Narratives for Children with Autism   47
    Joint Attention   48
    Peer-to-Peer Social Interaction   49
    Guiding Socialization and Imagination   49
    Reading Social Cues   49

Chapter Five: Classroom Environment   51

Classroom Environment for Preschoolers   51
    Physical Setting   51
        Learning Centers   51

                    Classroom Materials   52
                    Emphasize the Classroom as Community   52
            Time and the Classroom Environment   52
            The Social Environment   53
Classroom Environment for Children with Autism   53
            Physical Setting   53
            Example of a Child with Autism Having Difficulty Adjusting
                to the Classroom Environment   54
Strategies to Provide a Classroom Learning Environment   57
            Classroom Distractions   57
            Classroom Materials   57
                    Material Accessibility   57
                    Cultural Diversity in Materials   57
            Time and the Classroom Environment   58
            The Social Environment   58
                    Rest Area   58
                    Classroom Jobs   59

CHAPTER SIX: PLAY   61
Play for Preschoolers   61
            Play and Assessments   61
            Play and Development   61
            Social Play   62
Play for Children with Autism   63
            Play and Development   63
            Social Play for Children with Autism   64
            Example of a Child with Autism and Playing Difficulty   64
Classroom Strategies to Assist Play Development   66
            Social Play   66

CHAPTER SEVEN: GUIDANCE 69

Guidance for Preschoolers   69
Guidance for Young Children with Autism   70
    Developmental Delay and Guidance   70
    Sensory Integration and Guidance   70
    "Theory of Mind" and Guidance   71
    Communication and Guidance   72
    Example of Inappropriate Behavior in Autism   73
Classroom Strategies to Provide Positive Guidance   75
    Why This Behavior?   75
        Understanding Temperaments   75
        Helping Children Understand Feelings   76
    Feeling Safe   76
    We're All Friends   77
    Taking Responsibility for Challenging Behavior   78
    Managing Time and Guidance   78
    Encouraging and Reinforcing Positive Behavior   79

APPENDIX A   81
APPENDIX B   84
APPENDIX C   86
REFERENCES   87
ORGANIZATIONS SPECIALIZING IN AUTISM RESEARCH & INFORMATION   91
SUGGESTIONS FOR FURTHER READING   93
ANNOTATED BIBLIOGRAPHY   95

ABOUT THE AUTHOR   103

Foreword

Karen Roberts offers a rare gift to preschool teachers, who want to do the right thing for young children with autism but who are unsure about how to do that. This updated edition is also a gift for the parents who want their children to be included, but who are often confronted by staff with good intentions but little preparation for successfully adapting the preschool environment to meet the needs of children with autism. Roberts begins her book by stating, "In the scheme of things, raising a child with autism is really not so different. And as a preschool teacher, I believe teaching a child with autism should not be so different." She suggests that in the end, "every child needs to know he is accepted and belongs." Roberts brings the wealth of her experience as a parent of a child with autism, as well as her experience as a teacher of young children, to ensuring that other teachers can see how to realize that end in their classrooms.

Embracing Autism in Preschool has several unique features that make it an indispensible resource for classroom teachers and for parents, as well as for teacher preparation programs. Roberts has done meticulous work to include information on our most current understanding of autism, what it is, how it varies in expression among children, and implications for educational environments.

Yet, the book is not a book about autism; it is a book about inclusion. Roberts avoids continuously pointing out how children with autism are different, and, instead, frames her strategies within the context of what all young children need and how all young children develop. Her book itself is a model for inclusion. Further, Roberts has organized her book to incorporate our current best understanding of effective curriculum for all young children, including a focus on the power of play—a feature often left out when considering planning for young children with autism.

Roberts has also written a book that challenges us to ask, "What do I need to do to make this environment work for this child?" rather than, "What do I have to change about this child to make him work in this environment?" That orientation speaks volumes and goes a long way to ensure that a young child with autism will be successful and welcomed by his peers. Another feature that supports this orientation is Roberts' focus on guidance rather than behavior management. Roberts helps the reader to understand that what others may experience as challenging behavior or misbehavior might better be interpreted as "mistaken behavior," (Gartrell, 2004). She provides a theoretical basis for interpreting the challenging behaviors associated with autism, and offers practical ideas for positive guidance.

What ultimately makes this book so useful is the fact that Roberts offers many examples from the real life experiences of young children and their teachers. She also includes the voices of individuals with autism themselves. As such, we can see that inclusion works best when teachers, parents, and the children themselves see that they are all partners in the process.

A recent position statement of the Division for Early Childhood of the Council for Exceptional Children and the National Association for the Education of Young Children states:

> Early childhood inclusion embodies the values, policies, and practices that support the right of every infant and young child and his or her family, regardless of ability, to participate in a broad range of activities and contexts as full members of families, communities, and society. The desired results of inclusive experiences for children with and without disabilities and their families include a sense of belonging and membership, positive social relationships and friendships, and development and learning to reach their full potential. The defining features of inclusion that can be used to identify high quality early childhood programs and services are access, participation, and supports (DEC, NAEYC, April, 2009).

Roberts's book shows all of us how to make this vision a reality.

EVA K. THORP, ED.D.
Associate Professor, Early Childhood Education
George Mason University

Preface

> *"As human beings, our job is to help people realize how rare and valuable each one of us really is, that each of us has something that no one else has – or ever will have – something inside that is unique to all time. It's our job to encourage each other to discover that uniqueness and to provide ways of developing its expression.*
>
> —Fred Rogers

When this book was first published in 2010 there was an increased interest in autism. Since then, debates on treatments, therapies and experiments have increased in tandem with a rise in autism prevalence. It is my hope that this book update helps readers better understand the changes in autism diagnoses and treatments. For parents in your preschool program who wish to learn more about autism, I have written a book with the hope of answering the many questions they may have: *Let's Talk About Autism in Early Childhood.*

For general education preschool teachers who are including a child with autism in their classroom, the inclusionary strategies suggested here, easily generalized for all young children, have been successful for me in my preschool classes. In my experience teachers will find little need for added preparation and will realize that they have everything they need.

When the child with autism's family and education professional team determines that he/she is ready for a mainstream experience, *Embracing Autism in Preschool* will provide guidance on ways to modify current programs to be sure *all* children in the classroom become successful early learners. Although it provides an overview of the rapidly growing developmental disability of autism, *Embracing Autism in Preschool* focuses predominantly on classroom practices for inclusive success. As you will see in this book, inclusion is the law but it is also professionally satisfying and educationally appropriate.

As an educator and the parent of a child with autism, I am often asked, "So, what is it like to raise a child with autism?"

Parenting is a challenging experience. All parents are concerned for the welfare of their children. We want our children to be healthy and happy. We want them to have friends, and to enjoy life. We're willing to challenge anyone or anything which denies our child his rights or privileges. When this book was first written, my son was still navigating the public school system. He is now a healthy and happy adult. Through the years, our family has had good days and bad days. We've experienced difficult lessons and easier lessons. We've shared proud moments as well as disappointing moments. We worry about mistakes we've made in the past, and we worry about the inevitable mistakes we'll make in the future. We do what we have to do and hope we are not only doing the *right thing*, but the *best thing* for our child. We love each other dearly, and we cannot imagine our lives without each other.

In the scheme of things, raising a child with autism is really not so different from raising a child.

As a preschool teacher I believe teaching a child with autism should not be so different from simply teaching a child. A good preschool classroom is designed to meet the needs of the individual learner. Each child brings his unique cultural experiences to the classroom. Each child develops at a different pace. Each child learns differently. And, *every* child needs to know that he is accepted and that he belongs.

It is the challenge of all educators to understand differences and to meet the learning needs of each child within those differences. This is our professional discipline, and we welcome it.

Acknowledgements

"Our chief want in life is somebody who will make us do what we can."—Ralph Waldo Emerson

The Acknowledgements in the first edition of this book remain steadfast. I will always be grateful to my family, especially to my husband, David, and my son, Kevin, with whom I've shared this wonderful life journey. From the beginning I was supported by Burke United Methodist Church and their exemplary preschool program and staff. The first edition would not have been possible without encouragement from my professors at George Mason University, including Dr. Monimalika Day and Dr. Eva Thorp who have followed my educational journey from student to educator to author—sharing with others lessons they have taught. And, where would I be today, if I had not met Nancy Stodart at a conference? She offered to publish my first book and she and her husband, Richard, mentored me into an author's world. Thank you Fourth Lloyd Productions! To all of my co-teachers, especially Ana Hoover with whom I've continued to share the authors' journey, to my students, and to all the families who have shared their experiences and their children with me through the years, I am especially grateful. Thank you. I am truly blessed to have shared in your lives.

INTRODUCTION

Much has been learned about autism since the first edition of this book in 2010. Hopefully, this updated version will help to explain the changes made in the past ten years while acknowledging that the world of autism is in constant motion and our learning continues.

The early history of autism, however, can be reviewed without current fluctuations. For years autism was sorely misunderstood. Even after Leo Kanner and Hans Asperger began the first real studies of autism in the 1940's, children with autism continued to be institutionalized. This was due in great part to Bruno Bettelheim's autism claim. He suggested that children with autism were the result of extremely poor parenting, causing them to withdraw emotionally and have unusual behaviors. He recommended removal of the children from their parents, so the autism could be "cured". He called us, "refrigerator mothers". Twenty years later, in 1964, Bernard Rimland's research indicated that autism was due to abnormalities in the brain, not poor parenting (Bruey, 2004).

As research progressed, behavioral treatments became the treatment of choice in the 1970's. Finally, those with autism were no longer separated from their families, but they continued to be separated from the education mainstream. Today, with all of the current research in neurology, the media strives to keep up with the changes in autism research and discoveries. The rise in autism diagnosis has been referred to as a major health concern in the United States. Families touched by the disorder scramble to learn all that they can about therapies and education resources. All of these events are substantially changing—for the better—the way the public perceives autism.

Yet, in public schools all young children with autism have varied levels of ability, but they continue to be placed in segregated autism classrooms, non-categorical classrooms (along with children with varied disabilities), or they share their special education classroom with one or two neurotypical peers who serve as role models. This does not allow children with autism who are able to participate with same age peers the opportunity to learn the social skills practiced by every preschool child, nor does segregation from typically developing peers help them to develop skills which may further be challenged by an autism diagnosis. More importantly, it may be considered unlawful to segregate children to an unnatural and/or restricted environment when they are capable of learning in the mainstream.

So, where do general education preschool teachers fit in? As educators, it is time we take responsibility for helping families to understand that their child's autism label does not mean he/she will be excluded; rather, he/she is entitled to services and opportunities that we provide to typically developing peers. Exemplary preschool programs have all of the resources. This book contains tried and true strategies for including children with autism in a mainstream preschool classroom. The skills, the resources, the needs are here, but most importantly, it is the preschool teacher who has the heart to bring everything together and to succeed.

CHAPTER ONE
WHAT IS AUTISM?

AUTISM DEFINED

The Autism Society of America (ASA, 2010) defines autism as a complex developmental disability which typically appears during the first three years of life and affects a person's ability to communicate and interact with others. Researchers from the Kennedy Krieger Institute have demonstrated that a large number of children with autism can be diagnosed as early as fourteen months (Landa, Holman, Garret-Meyer, 2007). Those familiar with autism may also be familiar with the phrase, "If you know one person with autism, you know one person with autism" (Kluth, 2003, p. 2). This is because no two people with autism share the same experiences or abilities. Even those who share the same diagnosis do not necessarily share the same abilities, interests or challenges. In 2013, the American Psychiatric Association (APA), the organization responsibility for guiding professionals who diagnose brain disorders, updated the diagnosis criteria for autism. According to their latest standards in the Diagnostic and Statistical Manual of Mental Disorders (DSM-5), in order to receive a diagnosis for autism spectrum disorder (APA, 2013), a person must have:

A. Deficits in social communication and social interaction.

B. Restricted repetitive patterns of behavior, interests or activities in at least two of four areas:

    a. Stereotypical or repetitive movements;

b. Insistence on sameness;

   c. Highly restricted and/or fixative interests;

   d. Have either hypo- or hyper-sensory sensitivity or unusual interests in the sensory aspects of his environment.

C. Symptoms present in the early development period (even though the person may not show signs until he is older and struggling socially and/or has had time to learn strategies as he gets older to compensate for autism deficits).

D. Symptoms that cause significant impairment in the person's social life, in his occupation, or other important areas of his education and life.

E. Impairments are not explained by intellectual disability (ID) or global developmental delay. However, autism can occur with ID, so to distinguish between the two, social communication must fall below what would be expected for the child's general developmental level.

The DSM does suggest sensory aspects of the environment can be significantly challenging for children with autism. It is not uncommon for children with autism to present negative behaviors when they experience what I like to term, "sensory overload". However, it is important to note here that a diagnosis of autism does not mean a child will present negative behaviors (see chapter 7: Guidance). Yet, very often teachers are reluctant to include children with autism in their classrooms because the general public sometimes misunderstands autism and assumes every child with autism is subject to aberrant behavior which might cause them to be a danger to themselves or others in the community. We regret the pain this must have caused families in the past. As educators, it is our responsibility to move forward and to advocate for children with autism and their families by helping everyone to understand that autism is not defined by insubordinate behaviors.

The Autism "Spectrum"

Autism has often been referred to as a "spectrum disorder" because it affects each individual differently and because there is a wide range of abilities among those with autism (Bruey, 2004). In 2010, during the first writing of this book, autism was listed as five categories of diagnosis (Autism Society of America, 2007), including:
 (1) Autistic Disorder,
 (2) Asperger's Syndrome,
 (3) Childhood Disintegrative Disorder (CDD),
 (4) Rett's Disorder; and
 (5) Pervasive Development Disorder-Not Otherwise Specified (PDD-NOS).

When the APA updated the autism diagnosis criteria in the DSM-5, they eliminated the five autism diagnosis (APA, 2013). Instead of five separate diagnosis, autism is categorized according to "levels of severity":

- Autism, Level 1: Requires support: "Without supports in place, deficits in social communication cause noticeable impairments".

- Autism, Level 2: Requires substantial support: "Marked deficits in verbal and nonverbal social communication skills; social impairments apparent even with supports in place; limited initiation of social interactions; and reduced or abnormal responses to social overtures from others".

- Autism, Level 3: Requires very substantial support: "Severe deficits in verbal and nonverbal social communication skills cause severe impairments in functioning, very limited initiation of social interactions, and minimal response to social overtures from others" (p.30).

Although the five separate diagnosis were removed from the DSM as criteria for an autism diagnosis, many of the diagnosis can be found

elsewhere in the DSM. You may also continue to hear the diagnosis of Asperger's Syndrome because many characteristics of this earlier term closely fit the diagnosis of Autism Level 1.

HIGH OR LOW FUNCTIONING AUTISM?

When describing children with autism, it was once common for professionals to use the terms "high" functioning or "low" functioning autism. Since the new DSM diagnosis is presented in levels of severity, that terminology is not as common. Nonetheless, whatever the severity, it is best not to pigeonhole children by their level of function; rather, recognize each child as the individual he/she is with all of the gifts each has to share.

Dual Diagnosis in Autism

An autism diagnosis is often accompanied by other mental health or developmental disabilities (Kutscher, 2005). It is not uncommon for a child with autism to also have learning disabilities, intellectual disability, obsessive compulsive disorders, attention deficits, Tourette's syndrome, sensory integration problems, bipolar disorder or any combination of disorders. These shared diagnoses are termed "comorbidities" (Bruey, 2004). The combination of autism with other disorders makes it increasingly difficult to diagnose autism. This is especially true of preschool age children for whom initial testing of many disorders is not developmentally appropriate. Many children in preschool may actually have autism, but since they do not present obvious symptoms of the disorder they are not yet diagnosed.

How Prevalent Is Autism?

The Centers for Disease Control reports (2020) that one in every fifty-four persons over the age of eight is diagnosed with autism. They further report that while autism is not particularly prevalent among any racial, ethnic or educational level, it is four times more prevalent in boys than in girls. Autism is more common than pediatric cancer, diabetes, and AIDS combined. Between 1994 and 2006, the number of six to seventeen-year-old children labeled with autism in public schools increased from 22,664 to 211,610 children. These figures indicate that the number of public school students with autism has skyrocketed. Note that these numbers include only those children who have received a solid diagnosis of autism.

So what does this mean for preschool teachers? This means that if you have not had the privilege of having a child with autism in your classroom in the past, there's a very good chance you'll be teaching more than one child with autism in the very near future.

Learn More About Autism

This book does not include detailed information on autism spectrum disorders. Rather, its intent is to help preschool teachers realize that the abilities of many children with autism are equal to those of their neurotypical peers, and to provide strategies for preschool education in areas of challenge typical of young children with autism. You are encouraged to learn more about autism spectrum disorders (ASDs). Suggestions for further reading, an annotated bibliography, a contact list of organizations and websites specializing in autism research are included at the end of this book.

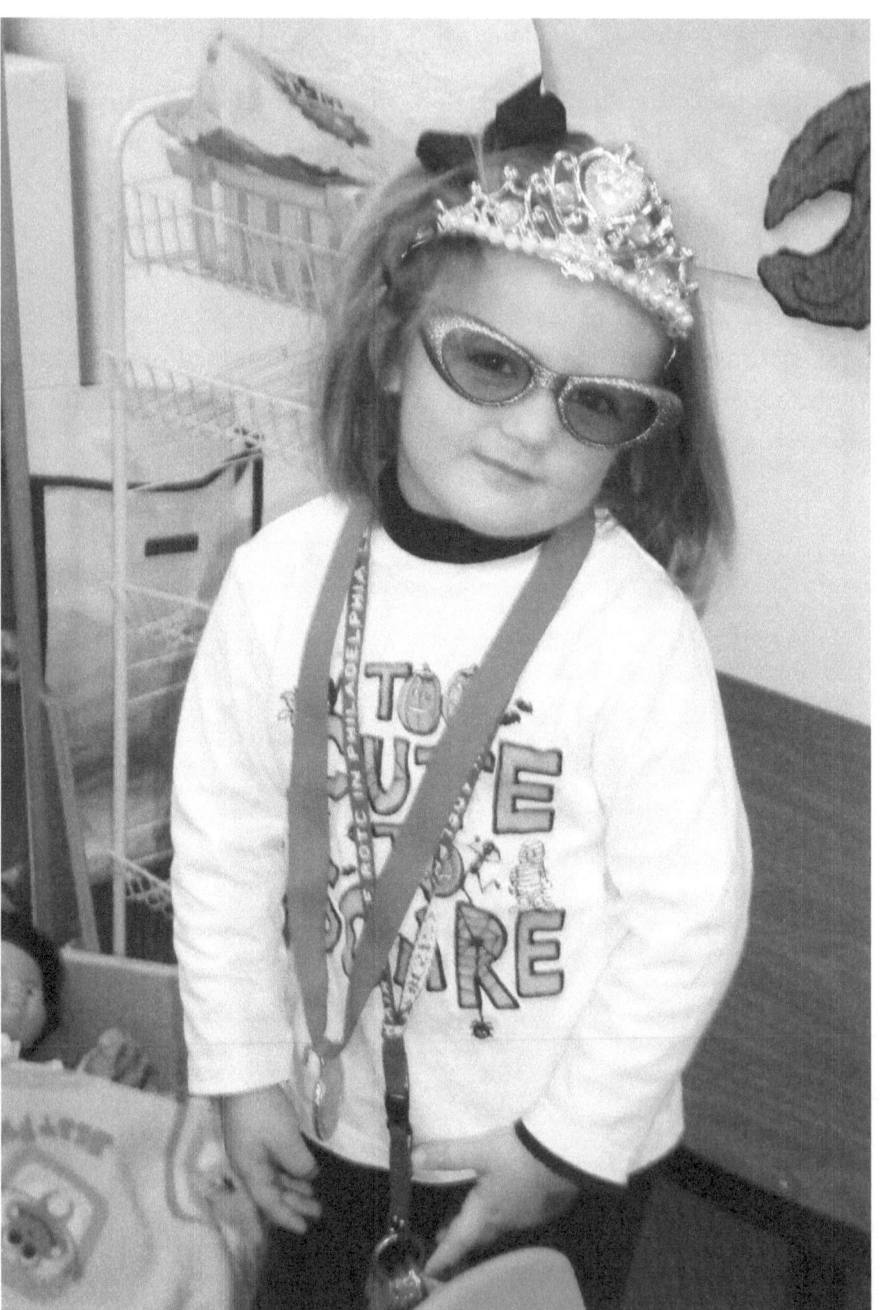

CHAPTER TWO
Why Inclusion?

Inclusion Is the Law

The Individuals with Disabilities Education Improvement Act (IDEA) of 1997 and its reauthorization, IDEA 2004, mandate that all children who have disabilities—which adversely affect their educational performance—are eligible for special education services (Department of Education, 2004). As indicated earlier, autism is defined as a disability in the Diagnostic and Statistics Manual (DSM) published by the American Psychiatric Association (APA, 2013), thereby making those with autism eligible for special education services. Additionally, any child with a disability is entitled to an Individualized Family Service Plan (IFSP) from birth and an Individualized Education Plan (IEP) once he/she enters the public school system. The law stipulates that any child receiving special education services must be educated in his least restrictive and most natural current environment. This means that any child with a disability must be included in settings with peers as much as possible, whether the natural setting is in the home, at a child care center or a school (Hooper & Umansky, 2004). In compliance with IDEA, these children are also entitled to disability services through their local government, school, or agency.

Inclusion Is Developmentally Appropriate

The Centers for Disease Control (CDC, 2007) report autism as the second most common serious developmental disability after intellectual disability. The CDC further emphasizes that public awareness of the increase in autism diagnoses is important and advises for the earliest intervention possible for any child who is suspected of having the disorder. *Studies reveal young children with autism who receive intervention before the age of five have a better chance of making progress enough to be included in general education classes* (Bruey, 2004). For a child with autism whose professional team deems the child ready for a mainstream experience, inclusion in a general education preschool program among same-age peers is an opportunity for a valuable life experience and provides a viable alternative in a least restrictive and natural learning environment.

INCLUSION IS THE BEST PRACTICE

Inclusion is the best practice for early childhood education because it focuses on educating young children among their peers as unique individuals. The National Association for the Education of Young Children (Bredekamp & Copple, 1997) describes best practices as individualizing instruction to the extent possible by: (1) what the teacher knows about the child's development; (2) what the teacher knows about each individual in her care; and (3) what the teacher knows about each child's culture and the social context in which the child lives and learns.

THE EXEMPLARY PRESCHOOL CLASSROOM

The Circle of Inclusion (2007), an organization which advocates for inclusion of all children with disabilities, emphasizes that an exemplary preschool classroom is designed to meet the needs of the individual child, whether or not the child has a disability. When a child's particular needs are not being met, the recommendation is to adapt the program to accommodate the child. Teachers need to remain flexible to various learning styles and children's specific individual needs.

A goal of this book is to support teacher flexibility. Early childhood educators are all familiar with developmentally appropriate practice. In developing a curriculum for the entire class, consideration is given to a range of learning styles. A solid curriculum is based on outcomes for the children—what we want them to learn—and how to accomplish those goals (Copple & Bredekamp, 2006). This is a strategy which is applied to the needs of every child, including those with autism. While we may not initially realize the impact, many of the strategies we adapt for children with autism reinforce learning styles for their typically developing peers and everyone in the classroom benefits. This should be our ultimate goal.

CHAPTER THREE
Language and Communication

> *The North American Encarta Dictionary defines communication as "The exchange of information between people, e.g., by means of speaking, writing, or using a common system of signs or behavior."*

Language and Communication in Preschoolers

Nekovei and Armis (2006) state that while language and communication represent a natural process, they require the ability to hear sounds and phrases and to make sense of their meaning. There must also be a desire to engage in communication/conversation with others. During preschool years (ages two to five) typically developing young children often do not have the vocabulary, nor do they fully understand how, to appropriately share or express feelings. Volkmar, Paul, Klin and Cohen (2005) inform us that as each year passes children are acquiring new vocabulary. Their sentence lengths increase. They begin to use language logically and imaginatively. By age five, children have acquired most of the sentence structure of their language—enabling them to communicate with peers and adults, to make requests, to make comments, and to choose appropriate speech based on the current topic of conversation.

Language and Communication in Autism

Pragmatic Language Delay

Language and communication present significant challenges to children with autism because the range of functioning abilities can vary from non-verbal to verbal competency. However, it is believed that across the levels of abilities in autism the one impairment that appears to impact all children is pragmatic language—the use of language in the social context.

Theory of Mind

A common challenge for those with autism is the inability to understand another person's perspective, referred to as "theory of mind" (Autism Society of America, 2007). The inability to understand another's perspective makes it difficult for children with autism to participate in shared communication.

Functional Communication

Along with pragmatic and theory of mind language delays, children with autism often use language which does not relate to the topic of conversation or current situation (Willis, 2006). This type of communication is termed, "non-functional communication", since it serves no purpose for a communicative exchange. Some children with autism use a type of non-functional communication termed "echolalia" (Volkmar, Paul, Klin & Cohen, 2005). Echolalia refers to the austistic child repeating what he has just heard. For instance, the teacher might say to the children, "Get your jackets on to go outside." The child with autism, while not necessarily aware of his utterances, may continue to repeatedly echo the phrase, "Get your jackets on to go outside. Get your jackets on to go outside . . ." Since language often develops with a very young child's attempt at speech by repeating phrases and words, Volkmar et. al (2005) suggest that echolalia may be an attempt by the autistic child to produce spontaneous speech as well as to aid them in acquiring language.

Receptive and Expressive Language

There is great variability in children with autism's receptive (understanding what is heard) and expressive (verbalizing) language abilities, as well as their attention system. Some children with autism spectrum disorders (ASDs) need verbal instructions to be accompanied by gestures, visuals, or repetition, while other children may just need more processing time.

Reciprocal Communication

Willis (2006) reports that some children with autism have difficulty initiating conversation unless they have something that highly motivates them. Rarely will children with autism communicate or initiate conversation to intentionally socialize. Ms. Willis explains further that for conversations to be understood by some children with autism, it must be concrete and literal. Because of their inability to read social cues, new social situations (reviewed in a later chapter), and abstract language, children with autism often face many reciprocal communicative challenges.

Example of a Child with Autism/Communication Deficits

Joey is a four year old child diagnosed with level one autism. He joined the general education preschool at the beginning of the school year. He is very communicative, although his communications are not always functional. While he has an extensive vocabulary, he does have a difficult time understanding another person's perspective (theory of mind). And when he is overly excited, nervous or upset, he sometimes includes echolalia in his speech.

Joey loves dinosaurs, so the teacher has purposefully made dinosaur manipulatives—toys and books—available in most centers so he has opportunities for reciprocal communication based on his knowledge and specific interest. The other boys in the class are in awe of Joey's knowledge of dinosaurs. They often pick up the plastic figures and ask the name of each dinosaur. Joey is always quick to respond in rote with clear specific information, providing not only the dinosaurs name but the dinosaur's period of life—whether it was carnivorous or vegetarian—it's exact dimensions, and with which dinosaurs it associated. Afterward, instead of engaging in further conversation or inviting others to play, Joey always returns to his isolated play, taking on the personality and voice of each individual dinosaur he holds.

This particular morning, after watching Joey play for a while, David asked if he could also play with the dinosaurs. Joey reluctantly nodded yes and pulled a few closer to himself as if to say, "These are mine only." As Joey conversed in the different voices from dinosaur to dinosaur, David stopped playing, watched, and listened. After a bit he laughed, and said, "You're funny!" Joey instantly broke into tears and punched David.

When the teacher investigated, Joey told her, "He said I'm funny. That's not nice to say. That boy said I'm funny." Joey had taken David's statement literally and did not understand his words were not meant to be hurtful name-calling comments.

The teacher asked David to stand next to Joey as she explained how she thought David was trying to say he enjoyed listening to Joey make all of those "fun-sounding voices"—not that Joey was a funny boy. David, teary-eyed, nodded in agreement, and Joey shrugged his shoulders, blandly replied, "Okay," and returned to the floor to play.

The teacher put her hand on Joey's shoulder and quietly reminded him that he hurt David when he punched him, and he should see if he's okay. Joey stood, and the teacher—hand over hand—placed Joey's hand on David's shoulder. Joey waited as the teacher prompted, "Ask him if he's okay." Joey said, "You okay?" David nodded yes, and moved to another center to play. Joey sat down and returned to his solitary play. Holding a dinosaur in each hand, he repeated over and over, "You okay. Yes, I okay. You okay? Yes, I okay…"

Classroom Strategies to Assist Development of Language and Communication

Provide Visual Supports

Rao and Gagie (2006, p. 26) report that visual supports
- are part of everyone's communication system,
- can attract and hold a student's attention,
- enable the student to focus on the message and reduce anxiety,
- make abstract concepts more concrete for the student, and
- help the student express his or her thoughts.

Picture cues can be generalized in the preschool classroom and used for visual schedules, song lists, games and other choices offered to the children during the day.

Visual Schedules

Preschool-age children function better with daily routines. Visual schedules support early literacy and sequencing skills while accommodating visual learners. Visual schedules help increase independence, assist with transitioning, and inform children in advance of potential changes in the daily schedule. A clip and copy sample of a daily schedule appears at Appendix A.

Picture Exchange Communication System (PECS)

Bondy and Frost (2002) emphasize that young children with autism often do not acquire communication skills at the rate of their typically developing peers. In self-contained autism classrooms for non-verbal children, professionals often use a Picture Exchange Communication System (PECS). PECS are picture icons which the student presents to the teacher in place of speaking. As the child learns to use

Language and Communication 37

the cards to represent an item, he can then begin to combine icons to represent full sentences (2002). PECS is also a behavioral intervention to teach less verbal children how to communicate intentionally with others by using pictures. PECS offers an expansive set of cards for sale. For the current edition of PECS, visit them on-line at www.pyramidproducts.com.

Enhancing Verbal Instruction

Children with autism typically do not learn by mere observation. They need specific and direct instruction. It is important to provide verbal instructions, along with gestures, visuals and repetition—while providing adequate time for processing and response. Children with autism have impaired attention systems, sometimes referred to as "stimulus overselectivity" (Lovaas, Schreibman, Koegel & Rehm, 1971). This means that while they may or may not respond to their name, they might immediately respond to a familiar tune or something else which highly motivates. This attention impairment hinders immediate responses, so teachers need to be mindful of providing the child with autism extra time to process material and then providing immediate positive feedback to responses. Providing immediate positive feedback motivates all children and is especially important for future successes of the child with autism.

Provide Instruction for All Learning Styles

Provide verbal, kinesthetic and visual instruction so that children with all combinations of learning styles have opportunities to participate.

Be Certain All Children Are Attentive and Engaged

Rocha, Schreibman and Stahmer (2007) explain that many children with autism have deficits in "joint attention"—which is defined as coordinating attention between an object and another person in the social context. They emphasize the importance of joint attention tasks for communicating and learning about the environment with another person. When instructing in the general education classroom, teachers should make sure all children are attending and provide adequate time for engagement. If a child's attention is elsewhere, he will not retain information. Because of their deficits in joint attention and eye gaze, children with autism especially need adequate time to process information.

Playing Games

Playing games engages children by involving them in taking turns, by encouraging them to use their words to request a turn and by finding ways to indicate to each other when it is someone else's turn. Sharing is often difficult for the earliest learners, and they often do not have a good concept of time for waiting. Consider using sand timers so the children can negotiate the time among themselves (see section on classroom environment).

Use Music to Communicate

Music motivates young children. Use familiar tunes and put words to the tunes when you want the children's attention. Use those familiar tunes along with song-gesture routines to encourage children with autism to imitate gestures. Pause to provide children the opportunity to fill in words to tunes and finger plays.

Using picture/communication cards for classroom music and allowing children to choose which song they would like to sing, also adds another opportunity for children to make choices.

Words made up to familiar songs can describe functions, such as "clean-up", or a change/transition in schedule and thus help not only to get childrens' attentions but also to give them time to prepare for the next activity.

READ! READ! READ!

Reading is Fundamental (RIF, 2008) reports that by reading aloud and encouraging children to read on their own, children become better readers, better listeners, and better students. Reading aloud also helps children build vocabulary and language skills, and helps them gain knowledge about the world around them. RIF also recommends that as the teacher reads aloud:
- she reads slowly with expression, using different voices for different characters;
- she follows the words with her fingers as she reads;
- she points to the pictures and says the names of objects and colors;
- she asks the children to describe pictures, repeat phrases in the story and predict what will happen next;
- she takes time to answer children's questions; and
- she reads a variety of books.

Manipulatives, Puppets and Humor

Use felt board story characters and puppets to accompany books and classroom discussions to encourage shared communication. Studies (Jenson, 2005) suggest that all children learn better when they have something visual and concrete to accompany a lesson. This is particularly true of children with autism. Laminate pictures to accompany stories and allow children to follow along on a felt board or match to like pictures on a wall board. Sequence or re-tell the story in pictures. Jenson (2005) further emphasizes that children respond well to humor so the teacher needs to be silly and fun to keep young children engaged.

Important Considerations for Communicating with Children

- Tell the children exactly what you want them to do, instead of instructing in the negative. For instance, if you want them to walk and they begin to run, say, "Walk." If you say, "Don't run," it takes more time for them to process the opposite of what you want them to do, thus they respond later than they would to the direct instruction.

• Tell them "what will be next when." For instance, say "When you finish cleaning up the block center, we will go outside." Rather than saying, "If you don't clean up those blocks, we won't go outside." More often than not, the schedule indicates you will be going outside regardless, so by stating the latter negative, you've also set yourself up for a lie.

• Instead of telling the children to "Be quiet," teach children the difference between outside and inside voices and noises. Then simply remind them to use an inside or outside voice when it is appropriate. For example, tell the children, "We share the building with other teachers and children. So, we don't disrupt them. We should walk in the building, and we should speak quietly and try not to make loud noises. We call that our 'inside voice.' When we go outside, we can run. We can speak loudly, yell and make loud noises. We call that our 'outside voice'. We can practice our voices today, and then we'll help each other remember which voice to use every day." Here is a fun strategy which is very successful when you are returning inside from outside play. Have the children "get rid of their outside voices" by yelling as hard as they can and "catch their loud voices/noises in their hands". Once they "catch the loud noise", tell them to put it in their pocket (or in their shoe if they don't have a pocket), and they can take it out again when they go back outside.

• Children with autism often have difficulty with eye gaze.

They often will not look directly in a person's eyes during an exchange of conversation. Without direct eye contact, it might appear that they are not attending, are not interested in, or do not hear the speaker. William Stillman (2003), a very successful adult with Asperger's Syndrome, explains the difficulty many people with autism have focusing on the conversation if they are also required to make direct eye contact. They become so distracted by the person's facial features and other things going on around them that they often lose track of the conversation. He further emphasizes how intrusive it felt, as a young person, whenever someone grabbed his chin so that he would look directly at them. Perhaps the best way to find out if any child is listening is to simply ask, "What did you hear me say?" This not only answers the question, "Did you hear me?", but if they can repeat what they heard, you also know they understood what you said.

CHAPTER FOUR
Social Skills in Autism

"Social relationships are an important context for learning. Each child has strengths or interests that contribute to the overall functioning of the group. When children have opportunities to play together, work on projects in small groups, and talk with other children and adults, their own development and learning are enhanced. Interacting with other children in small groups provides a context for children to operate on the edge of their developing capacities. The learning environment enables children to construct understanding through interactions with adults and other children."

—National Association for the Education of Young Children, 2004

Social Skills For Preschoolers

Social Reciprocity

Social reciprocity is a major educational goal for all preschool children. As the National Association for the Education of Young Children (NAEYC, 2004) indicates above, it is important to remember that each child brings to the classroom unique gifts to share.

Social reciprocity is a challenging deficit for the child with autism. Children with autism typically do not learn through observation and modeling. Rather, they require direct instruction to develop the skills necessary for social interaction (Howley & Arnold,

2005). Because the major goals of preschool educators include direct instruction in social skills, all children are learning together:
- how to be part of a group,
- how to make friends,
- how to understand and follow rules and routines,
- how to express empathy,
- how to follow directions.

Also importantly, there is the goal of finding ways to help students to properly self-regulate behavior.

Placed in an inclusive preschool environment, children with autism can receive guidance from teachers and learn directly from same-age peers, thus providing them the social network beneficial for every child's social and emotional growth (Kluth, 2003).

Joint Attention and Social Sharing

Coordinating attention between an object and another person in a social context is referred to as "joint attention" (Rocha, Schreibman & Stahmer, 2007). Joint attention tasks are necessary for children to communicate and share information as well as emotional meaning with friends and caregivers. Throughout their younger years, children typically learn many of their social skills and attitudes when they are modeled by adults and other children.

The child with autism, however, is challenged by coordinating attention between an object and another person in a social context (Rocha, Schreibman & Stahmer, 2007), and modeling does not work for them. They generally do not learn by mere observation. They need specific and direct instruction.

Reading Social Cues

By seven months of age, infants smile at a familiar face, laugh, and express caution when looking at a stranger's face. Through body language and facial expressions, most typically developing children can interpret how another person is feeling.

Deficits in gaze behaviors and other non-verbal ways to socially communicate and share information are typical of children on the autism spectrum (Volkmar, Paul, Klin & Cohen, 2005). Because they often do not understand and participate themselves in communication through body language and facial expression, some children with autism are unable to read social cues and may need help interpreting another's cues.

Example of a Child with Autism and Social Skills Deficits

Drew is a five year old recently diagnosed with autism level one. He has been part of the mainstream preschool for the past two years. Each morning he arrives and follows a routine of putting all of his belongings in his cubby, hanging up his jacket, and moving directly to play with magnets in the science center. The teacher is aware of his current fascination with gravity, space and magnetic forces. She often asks one of his peers if he would like to join Drew and her in the centers he chooses. While Drew is always pleased to have a friend join him, he often doesn't know what to do. The teacher is sensitive to his anxiety and understands that he often needs prompting for peer play.

This particular day, the teacher asked Mark to join them in the science center. Drew had spent so much time with the magnets that with little teacher prompting he was able to show his peer, Mark, how to make them attract and repel each other. Pleased with Drew's progress in making reciprocating conversation, the teacher left the two of them to play. After about five minutes of additional parallel play, Drew began dropping the magnets harder and harder—making them repel and bounce off of each other onto the table—as he softly repeated, "bouncy, bouncy, bouncy." Upon seeing the reaction of the magnets, Mark forced his pile onto Drew's pile of magnets. Magnets then began repelling off the table as both boys repeated, "bouncy, bouncy, bouncy". Before long, item after item was being bounced out of the science center to various areas of the classroom. The noise level rose quickly with Mark's uncontrollable laughter and Drew's howling with laughter and screaming, "bouncy, bouncy, bouncy," while flapping his arms.

The teacher intervened, reminding Drew and Mark to use indoor voices. She further instructed them to begin picking up the toys around the room. Drew continued to laugh and attempted to help with the cleanup. However, he continued repeating "bouncy, bouncy, bouncy," while trying to bounce toys, rather than place toys back into place. At one point he picked up a wooden block and threw it hard onto the floor. The block bounced off the floor hitting one of the other children on the back of the head. She began to scream and cry.

The room was suddenly quiet. Most of the children in the room stopped what they were doing and stared in the teacher's direction. Initially distracted by the abrupt silence, Drew stopped. However, oblivious to the reason the little girl was crying, he quickly returned to dancing around, bouncing toys, and repeating, "bouncy, bouncy, bouncy..."

The teacher put her hand on Drew's shoulder and asked him if he knew what had just happened. Drew giggled and answered, "I bounced it." The teacher continued in a calm voice, pointing to the little girl. "The toy did bounce, you are right. However, when it bounced it hit Laura. She is crying. That hurt her."

Drew followed her point and continued to giggle. Unconcerned, he looked around the room to see what his friend Mark was doing, as he whispered to himself, "bouncy, bouncy, bouncy". The teacher continued, "Drew, if someone threw a block at you and hit you on the back of the head, what do you think would happen?" Drew grew angry at the suggestion and answered, "I would be angry. I would cry!"

Hoping she had made her point, the teacher directed Drew to take care of his friend and be sure she was okay.

Classroom Strategies to Assist Social Skills Development

Social Narrative and Picture Books in the Mainstream

There are many types of social narratives. In the mainstream preschool classroom, social narratives may be presented in a fictitious manner to address important social areas. Children's book publishers provide an array of social narratives which emphasize ways to share; how to join in play; how to take turns or wait in line; the importance of keeping things cleaned up; ways to self-regulate behaviors; and recognizing differences. A list of favorite picture books for young children which address specific areas of social competence can be found at Appendix B.

Social Narratives for Children with Autism

Although social narratives can be written to help children with or without disabilities to learn routines, to address behavior issues and social skills, to learn academic skills in a social setting, and to describe a social situation (Soenksen & Alper, 2006), they can be very helpful with children who have deficits in auditory/language processing, abstract thinking, or difficulty sustaining attention. Children often benefit from writing stories together in the classroom with its abundance of child-specific information.

Once a teacher becomes aware of particular student challenges, she can develop social narratives with step by step instructions of children developing those social skills. Ideally, the social narrative would include pictures of the child for whom the book is written.

Since children with autism do not generally learn from modeling, they need more concrete direct instruction. Social narratives provide the teacher an opportunity to provide direct instruction in simple story form. As Willis (2006) notes, social narratives help the child with autism to predict others' behaviors in social situations and help the child learn what is expected of him in a particular situation (p. 161). An example social narrative that appears in Appendix C was written for a child who needed help communicating basic greetings. This narrative was developed using guidelines in Carol Gray's (2000) book, *The New Social Story Book*. Gray's book, which is included in this manual in the Suggestions for Further Reading, is an excellent reference for helping to develop social narratives for younger children.

Joint Attention

Coordinating attention between an object and another person in a social context, referred to as joint attention, is a necessary skill for children to socially share their experiences. Making social interaction meaningful and finding ways to motivate the child are critical components of joint attention (Koegel & Koegel, 2006). Because the preschool classroom contains a myriad of age-appropriate toys, games and activities, it is a natural place for all children to learn to play together and share information. Teachers can facilitate joint attention for children with autism by following their interest leads and by physically pointing out areas of interest. Koegel (2006) suggests that putting highly motivational items slightly out of reach of the child with autism enables him to use his words or non-verbal communication to ask for the items. To encourage peer-to-peer social interaction, the teacher can prompt another child to assist the child with autism, if he wants something of interest—thus initiating joint attention among peers. Non-verbal gestures—such as pointing, reaching, and nodding—should be used frequently to facilitate prompting of all children and to provide them opportunities to respond.

Peer-to-Peer Social Interaction

Social interaction and responding to others should be taught to and encouraged for all children (Koegel & Koegel, 2006). Peer to peer play must be based on mutual interest. Since the child with autism will rarely initiate play, the teacher must observe the child's interests and can match them to at least one other child to act as 'peer model' in the classroom. The teacher can facilitate play by inviting a child to join her play along with another child. She can model questions and conversations and coach the peer model child to converse with the child with autism. Koegel (2006) suggests this shift from teacher as facilitator to peer as facilitator aids further in the intervention of age-appropriate language, social, and play skills for the child with autism.

Guiding Socialization and Imagination

Pamela Wolfberg has developed a manual on the art of guiding children's socialization and imagination, entitled, *Peer Play and the Autism Spectrum* (2003). This "integrated play group" manual is based on a process in which children participate in mutually-valued activities with the support of other children who vary in social skills. This manual is a wonderful resource for teachers wishing to investigate strategies for peer-to-peer social interaction in the classroom. Teachers must be mindful that typically developing peers need coaching and reinforcement to be good peers in an inclusive setting.

Reading Social Cues

While young children can usually read social cues from others, they often do not know how to express their own feelings. Because of challenges in theory of mind and very often a lack of eye gaze, children with autism do not read social cues. Therefore, the classroom teacher can facilitate social interaction for all of her students by giving them words to express their feelings and teaching them the meaning of non-verbal conversation. For instance, during picture book stories on emotion, the teacher can focus on the emotion of happiness and point to a "smiling child" photo before asking all of the children to smile. Have the children look at one another to see what a smiling face looks like, thereby establishing a clue for the emotion of happiness.

CHAPTER FIVE
Classroom Environment

The National Association for the Education of Young Children emphasizes the importance of recognizing the classroom environment as a "community of learners." They elaborate the importance of community by stating that "In a caring community of learners, everyone feels...
- *I belong here.*
- *I am safe.*
- *I matter, and everyone else in the group matters too.*
- *When we have problems, we can work them out.*
- *Together we can do great things."*
(Copple and Bredekamp, 2006, p. 27)

Classroom Environment for Preschoolers

Physical Setting

The first recognized components of a classroom environment are the physical characteristics of the classroom. These characteristics include size and use of classroom space, set up of the classroom, availability of classroom materials, and the classroom furnishings (Hull, Goldhaber & Capone, 2002).

Learning Centers

The best learning centers provide a rich learning environment.

Classroom space should be divided to accommodate small and large group activities. While large open spaces provide opportunities for physical activity, smaller centers give children ample opportunities to engage in social play and conversation. Areas intended for noisier play should be located with similar activity areas, just as quiet areas should be in the same vicinity of other quiet activity centers. There should be a quiet area of the room designated specifically for children when they need some time to themselves.

Classroom Materials

Classroom materials need to be safely accessible for children. Materials should support pretend play, facilitate engagement and social interaction among children, and be age-appropriate. When new materials or games—which require a set of instructions or rules—are introduced to the classroom, teachers should provide instruction on how to correctly play with the materials.

Emphasize the Classroom as Community

To emphasize the classroom as a community, each child should have an area for personal belongings which are transported to and from home. Children should be encouraged to provide art work, pictures, and materials they've made that can be posted on walls and placed in learning centers. Photographs of children throughout the classroom also help establish a feeling of belonging to the classroom community.

Time and the Classroom Environment

Young children depend on routines to process the structure of their days. The classroom daily schedule should provide children with a list of activities that must occur on schedule daily. Children should be informed of significant changes in the schedule well in advance of the alternate activities. Likewise, when children are engaged in activities that provide rich learning experiences, it is important that teachers remain flexible and make necessary changes in the schedule to facilitate those experiences and allow students time to aborb them. Teachers should always let children know in advance of the next activity by telling them how much time they have remaining to play.

The Social Environment

The social environment in the preschool classroom provides the atmosphere which influences the way children feel about themselves, their friends, and their teachers (Hull, Goldhaber & Capone, 2002). Teachers should make the effort to greet each child and help the child comfortably settle into the classroom. Children must know they are safe, cared for, and welcome, as soon as they enter the classroom daily.

CLASSROOM ENVIRONMENT FOR CHILDREN WITH AUTISM

Physical Setting

Children with autism function well in a well-structured preschool classroom environment. The physical setting which includes choices in learning centers, the emphasis on a classroom community, set daily schedules, classroom rules, and the emphasis teachers place on helping each child develop self-worth, are all fundamentals of an exemplary preschool program which benefit children with or without autism. However, children with autism are often easily distracted and are easily overstimulated by escalating noise levels, changing schedules and the anxiety of trying to make sense of the social environment. Therefore, strategies or accommodations must be made so they can comfortably function within the classroom.

Example of a Child with Autism Having Difficulty Adjusting to the Classroom Environment

Martin is a four year old child diagnosed with autism level three. His parents currently enrolled him in a private preschool five mornings a week. He attends a special education preschool class in the afternoon. Since he is not yet comfortable separating from his family in the morning, his father spends fifteen minutes with him each morning and settles him in a learning center as the other children arrive.

This particular morning, after his father left, Martin sat teary-eyed in the quiet center in a corner of the classroom library. He understands that he can go to the quiet center anytime he wants to be by himself. After about ten minutes, he pulled a book off of the shelf and turned the pages. The teacher carefully made her way toward Martin. Martin watched her approach. She sat next to him and asked if they could read together. Martin nodded. The teacher understands when Martin is upset because he gestures but rarely speaks.

She sat down and began to read, pointing to the pictures and waiting for Martin's reaction, giving him ample time to respond. Just as he was beginning to smile and feel comfortable the fire alarm rang.

The noise startled him. He grabbed the teacher's arm, placed his hands over his ears, screamed for his father, and darted toward the door. One teacher followed behind him trying to calm him as the other teacher gathered the children to exit the building. By the time everyone got to the exit, Martin was screaming so loudly, in so much pain, that no one could gain his attention. Outside, the teacher attempted to hold him as he screamed. The alarm stopped, and Martin stopped briefly to listen, then returned to a sobbing cry. The teacher held him, reassuring him everything is okay, and letting him know she understood it was a loud noise. The Principal gave the "all clear" for students and teachers to return to the classroom.

Martin was determined NOT to return to the room. He was still shaking and sobbing. While the other children returned inside, the teacher continued reassuring Martin all would be okay, and suggested they go in and get a drink of water so he might feel better. He agreed, but entered the building with caution. The remainder of the day, every little sound had Martin on alert.

Later, when his father arrived, he began crying all over again. As his father picked him up the teacher explained the morning's events. Martin held tightly to his father and sobbed. His father patted his back and said, "That must have been scary, it was so loud." Martin nodded. The teacher told Martin she was looking forward to him returning the next day so they could finish reading the book together. Martin nodded.

Strategies to Provide a Classroom Learning Environment

Classroom Distractions

Willis (2006) suggests defining learning centers with pictures. Many children with autism are often easily distracted and overstimulated. If the child with autism seems distracted by visuals, it is recommended that posters and pictures on the walls be kept at a minimum, unless they serve the purpose of reinforcing the current lesson.

Classroom Materials

Material Accessibility

Classroom materials should be safely accessible to the children. However, Koegel (2006) suggests putting items which highly motivate slightly out of reach of the child with autism so that he/she has multiple opportunities to use his/her words or non-verbal communication to ask for the items. Additionally, so that the child with autism is not overwhelmed and overstimulated by too many choices, it is recommended that materials with several pieces be kept in clearly marked containers with lids, so that only one container can be accessed at a time and still provide the child multiple opportunities to communicate his/her choices.

Cultural Diversity in Materials

To emphasize the classroom as community, classroom materials must reflect diverse cultures (Epstein, 2007). Art areas should include paper and crayons in different skin tones and should be open to encourage art which children can recognize from their own communities. Block and construction areas should contain vehicles representing different types of jobs, diverse building materials and unusual animals. Books should be multicultural as well as some written in languages which reflect children's home language. The house area should contain multiracial dolls, foods from different cultures, and props and dress-ups which reflect cultures and disabilities. Music in the classroom should reflect many cultures. The science area should include photos of the world's plant life and animal wildlife which are representative of real life.

Time and the Classroom Environment

Children with autism are especially dependent on daily routines. They often do not adjust well to changes and need to know well in advance of alternate activities so they can process the change, as well as prepare themselves for the change. Issues of time are difficult for all young children because they have not yet developed a concept for minutes and hours. Many school supply stores carry large sand timers in one, three and five minute increments. An investment in a sand timer for the classroom gives young children the visual of the passing time. For instance, the sand timer can be placed on the table and the teacher can announce, "We have five more minutes to play. When the sand timer is finished, it will be time to clean up." Sand timers also provide guidance to children when they are waiting for a turn to share a toy as in, "You may have a turn on the bike when Joyce is finished. Joyce is going to ride it for three minutes. It will be your turn when the sand timer is finished."

The Social Environment

Rest Area

Children with autism do not know how to join in imaginative play, nor do they understand how to engage in social play or read social cues (see Chapter 4: Social Skills in Autism). These social deficits make it extremely difficult for the child with autism to fit into the social environment. Simply by being included in the classroom environment children with autism have to work constantly to "fit in" the social environment. One can imagine how exhausting it must be. Therefore, it is critical that these children understand that there is a place in the room where they can go to separate themselves from the group whenever they need some time to themselves.

Classroom Jobs

Children enjoy active participation in the classroom environment. As indicated earlier, a space for personal belongings helps the children realize everyone belongs. Another way to build upon the classroom community is to make sure every child in the room has a job for the day. Jobs can be chosen among a myriad of classroom tasks for the day, including: lunch/snack helpers, flag holder, teacher helpers, weather reporter, calendar helper, schedule helper, clean up time announcer, line leader, chair helper, group game leaders, or any other task done routinely each day. It is important that each child has a job each day in order to feel some ownership and belonging to the classroom community. For the child with autism, pairing him with a peer for jobs may be helpful if he needs more guidance.

CHAPTER SIX
Play

"There are no rules of architecture for a castle in the clouds."

— G.K. Chesterton

Play for Preschoolers

Adults fill a young child's world with directions on behavior, specific daily routines, language, and social interaction. During play, a child can play spontaneously without adult supervision and direction. Children then take what they have learned and apply it to every domain of their play. The most effective play experiences from which children learn about the world around them are those experiences chosen by the child. Play experiences must be pleasurable for all children, totally engaging, flexible, imaginative, and changing. During such play, the children make the rules, they change the rules and they decide what is real and what is pretend (Wolfberg 2003).

Play and Assessments

Play facilitates the assessment process when children are actively engaged in activities they chose. During play, teachers can observe a child's developmental status across all domains—social, emotional, motor, language and communication, and cognitive.

Play and Development

Research (Hirsh-Pasek & Golinkoff, 2003) indicates that play promotes creativity, problem solving, and intellectual growth. Play also helps develop social and emotional skills. Teachers should act as facilitators for play by providing choices.

Play also reinforces development because it provides opportunities for new learning experiences (Johnson, Christie & Wardle, 2005). Early childhood theorist, Jean Piaget, believed that play is the most important avenue for learning since children create their own understanding of what's going on instead of relying on an adult's instruction. Piaget believed play is learned in stages as part of a child's developmental process (Johnson, Christie & Wardle, 2005):

- **Stage 1:** Practice play—which are simple sensory motor activities such as sucking, opening and closing hands, mouthing, patting, reaching and kicking. Children are in stage one of play from birth to age two.
- **Stage 2:** Symbolic or make-believe play—which consists of developing make-believe scenarios, taking on another's role or personality such as superheroes or adult roles/careers or using props to represent materials (i.e., a wood block becomes a cell phone). Children are in stage two of play from age two to age eleven or twelve.
- **Stage 3:** Games with rules—which is the most advanced stage of play. Children start playing games with rules around age eleven or twelve. At this point the games are played by the rules, or by the rules the entire group agrees upon. After age eleven or twelve, the games are set with rules. This is the stage of play which bridges into adulthood.

Social Play

Early childhood theorist, Lev Vygotsky, believed that all learning takes place in a social context (Bodrova & Leong, 1996). He believed that children learn when adults provide guidance with suggestions and ideas and provide children ample time to apply those ideas and skills to their play (Mooney, 2000). Sharing experiences and communicating those experiences to others forces the child to think logically and to speak clearly so his ideas can be understood. Teachers can support children's social learning by providing varied opportunities for children to work and play together.

PLAY FOR CHILDREN WITH AUTISM

Play and Development

Children on the autism spectrum do not follow the traditional developmental play path which is intertwined with language, social skills, and cognition (Wolfberg, 2003). This stands to reason since language and social skills are two areas of major impairment for children with autism, and autism is a developmental disorder. Piaget's stages one and two of play might therefore be described differently for a child with autism:

• **Stage 1:** *Practice play*—Simple sensory motor activities such as sucking, opening and closing hands, mouthing, patting, reaching and kicking. This type of play is more common with children on the autism spectrum who are often more interested in manipulating objects and exploring their senses by mouthing, spinning, and lining up objects (Wolfberg, 2003). They often develop inappropriate patterns of play with a particular toy. For instance, a child may play with trucks and cars, but turn them upside down and watch as the wheels spin over and over. These physical types of play progress into repetitive running, jumping, spinning, and bouncing—often continuing well past the two year developmental stage of typical practice play.

• **Stage 2:** *Symbolic or make-believe play*—Developing make-believe scenarios, taking on another's role or personality such as superheroes or adult roles/careers or using props to represent materials (i.e., a wood block becomes a cell phone). Children on the autism spectrum do not spontaneously engage in symbolic or make-believe play. While they might be able to play with trucks and dolls, their play is often the same, with the same toys in the same learning center. Their difficulty in engaging make-believe play may be a combination of some children's inability to understand another person's perspective, referred to as "theory of mind" (Autism Society of America, 2007), a lack of motivation, poor communication skills, and inadequate social skills.

Social Play for Children with Autism

Since many children with autism translate literally, they do not often understand when other children engage in pretend play. They may simply not know how to join in imaginative play (Willis, 2006). Children with autism generally do not share their experiences, imitate others, or respond to emotions.

Example of a Child with Autism and Playing Difficulty

Matthew is a three year old who is transitioning into a general education preschool after having received government services for the past year. Matthew has a diagnosis of autism level three. His language was developing typically until he was two years old. Since that time he has discontinued speaking all but a few words, "Mama, for his Mother, Da for his Dad and Cu when he wants something to eat or drink. He is currently using some sign language. His family and social workers hope his inclusion in a classroom with same-age peers will encourage communication and help him to develop some social skills.

Like most days, this morning Matthew played in the manipulative center with two peers. He had replaced the puzzles the teacher left on the table with a set of plastic gears, much to the chagrin of his peers. One of the two girls looked at Matthew and said, "Matt, you always get out the gears. I want to play with the puzzles." Matt continued constructing the same square of spinning gears he constructed every time he played in the center. The two girls started to leave the center when the Teacher intervened.

"Matthew," she said, "Why don't we work on this puzzle together?" Matthew continued with the gears as if he were not listening. "How about we put the puzzle together, and when we're finished we will all build a bunch of gears bigger than the puzzle. Without acknowledging the teacher's suggestion Matthew stopped what he was doing, took each gear piece and put it back in the box and onto the shelf.

The teacher pulled out the puzzle and the girls returned to the table. Matthew watched them put the puzzle together until the teacher put two pieces in his hand. She helped him find the place for the pieces, and they finished the puzzle.

As soon as they put the puzzle away, Matthew pulled out the box of gears and put together the same square of spinning gears. The teacher added two more squares. He hesitated but continued to spin his original set. Two other children joined in building. Matthew stepped back, continued to spin his own square, and played parallel to his peers as they added gears and gadgets to the construction. In an effort to show him how he might add to his set, the teacher added a gear to rotate his set. He removed the gear so that he could play with his set solitarily.

Classroom Strategies to Assist Play Development

Social Play

As indicated earlier in the social skills section of this book, social reciprocity is a major educational goal for all preschool children. On the other hand, social reciprocity is a challenging deficit for the child with autism. Since children with autism typically do not learn through observation and modeling, they require direct instruction to develop the skills necessary for social interaction and social play (Howley & Arnold, 2005). Placement in an inclusive environment where they can receive guidance from teachers and directly from same-age peers provides those with autism the social network beneficial for every child's social and emotional growth (Kluth, 2003). If a child is new to the class, consider who might be a good peer buddy for the child to help him become familiar with the classroom, the other children, and classroom routines.

Teachers can facilitate social interaction by initiating and guiding specific play activities and games based on the child's play preferences. In her book, *Teaching Young Children with Autism*, Willis (2006, p.24) outlines the following suggestions when teaching play strategies to a child with autism.

- Introduce one new toy or activity at a time. Too much change can be overwhelming.
- Show him each step. Then, ask him to repeat it after you.
- Start off with very short periods of structured play. Then, make the time longer as the child learns to tolerate the activity.
- Talk about the activity and use the appropriate language level for each child. Be animated and use a happy approach by saying such things as, "Wow, I just love rolling the ball to you!" or "You built that tower so high, isn't this fun?"...
- When teaching a new skill, use the child's name and tell him what will happen.

- Next, show him or model the steps in the activity, and encourage the child to try the activity on his own.
- Make sure every play activity is FUN and rewarding for the child. Remember, the main reason children play is because it is fun.

CHAPTER SEVEN
GUIDANCE

"Our sons and daughters aren't robots that need to be controlled. They are children who need to learn how to get along in the world. They need the ability to communicate in ways that will enable them to have their needs met. And we need to listen to what they tell us. Their behavior doesn't need to be perfect. It doesn't even need to 'look' like other children's behavior. Children with physical disabilities move differently than other children and that's just fine. It's also fine if children with behavioral disabilities behave differently than other children" (Snow, 2001, p. 342).

GUIDANCE FOR PRESCHOOLERS

Guidance issues seem to dominate the interest of most preschool teachers. Attendance is always heavy at professional development sessions on applied behavior analysis, positive discipline strategies, variations of time out, and one, two, three, magic. The Division for Early Childhood (DEC, 1999) informs that many young children engage in challenging behaviors in the normal course of development. Occasionally, however, there will be a child who does not respond to intervention. Developmental specialists (Kaiser & Rasminsky, 1999) define challenging behaviors as:

• any behavior that interferes with children's learning, development and success at play;

- behavior that is harmful to the child, other children, or adults;
- behavior that puts a child at high risk for later social problems or school failure.

More specifically, challenging behavior includes hitting, pinching, biting, kicking, spitting, bullying, teasing, ignoring rules, excluding other children, calling names, destroying property, or more commonly seen actions such as not sharing, or having a temper tantrum. Research (Kaiser & Rasminsky, 1999) further indicates that physical aggression starts at about nine months and peaks between twenty-seven and twenty-nine months. By the age of three, most children have learned how to use more socially-appropriate means of having needs met. Naturally, most children exhibit challenging behaviors beyond three when they are afraid, sad, angry, anxious, or otherwise upset. *Generally, children misbehave when they want something, or they want to avoid something.*

Guidance for Young Children with Autism

Developmental Delay and Guidance

Learning how to use socially appropriate means for meeting one's needs is developed around age three. Because there are developmental delays, children with autism are at a higher risk for developing challenging behaviors. Willis indicates (2006) that children with autism will often exhibit the same behaviors as their peers, but a temper tantrum may last longer or the behavioral reaction might be more intense. However, this does not mean challenging behaviors are evident in all children with autism.

Sensory Integration and Guidance

Children with autism often exhibit unusual behaviors such as hand flapping, twirling, covering their ears and screaming, which may place them at risk for social problems. Some children with autism have sensory integration deficits. Research (Grandin, 2005) indicates that children with autism often do not have the ability to integrate incoming sensory information well enough to choose on which stimulus to attend. This is where we get the stereotypical picture of the child with autism covering his ears and screaming. A specific sound can actually be a painful experience. Some children with autism are also quite sensitive kinesthetically and may prefer not to be touched or hugged. Temple Grandin (2005), a professional adult with Aspergers Syndrome, shares the following:

> *"Tactile stimulation for me and many autistic children is a no-win situation. Our bodies cry out for human contact, but when contact is made, we withdraw in pain and confusion. It wasn't until I was in my mid-twenties that I could shake hands or look directly at someone (pp. 36-37)."*

Interesting research (Norton 2013) suggests that in addition to over-reacting and under-reacting to senses, it is believed that many children with autism may actually tangle or mix their senses—or have what is called, "synesthesia." For instance, when they see a particular color, they may also be able to taste or smell the color. Teachers need to understand and be acutely aware of sensory integration deficits for the child with autism in their care, since many challenging behaviors stem from responses to those deficits.

'Theory of Mind' and Guidance

Because they have deficits in 'theory of mind' or understanding another person's perspective, children with autism are often unaware of a misstep. They often say or do things that are inappropriate. Not reading social cues well, they might not understand if someone is upset and they may overstep a boundary. Children with autism are also quite literal and may interpret incorrectly something someone said to them and act quickly in their own defense. These deficits can lead to inappropriate behavior and put them at risk socially.

Communication and Guidance

Many children with autism have communication deficits. When they struggle to verbalize and are unable to sufficiently communicate their needs, they may become frustrated and act inappropriately.

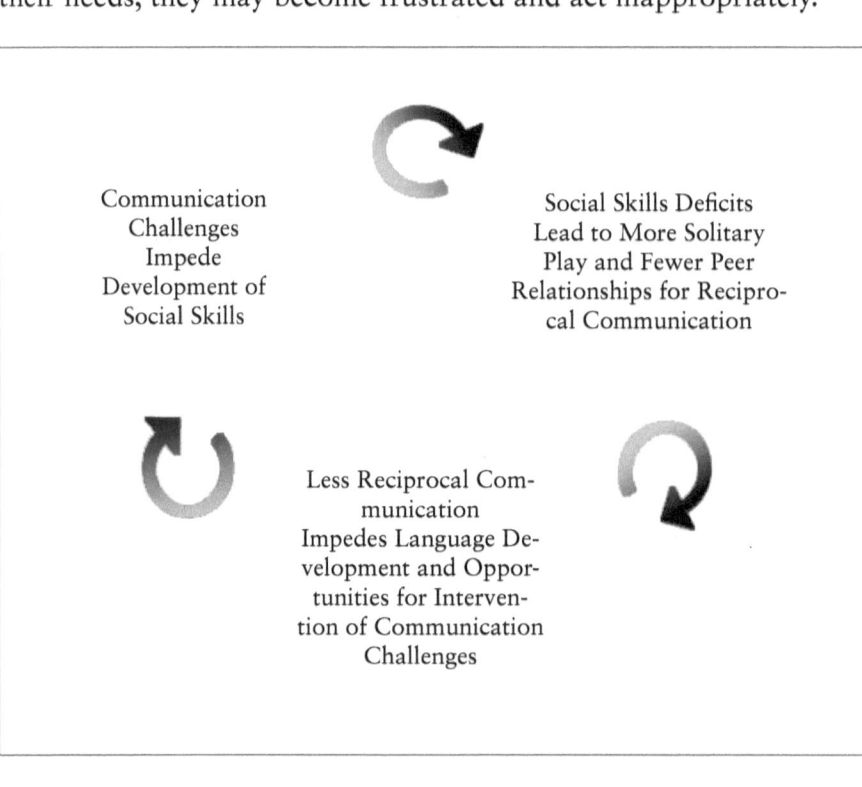

Language and communication development is dependent—in great part—on social experiences. When children have social skills deficits they tend to play more solitarily. Solitary play leads to fewer peer relationships and less opportunities for reciprocal communication. Less reciprocal communication impedes language development and opportunities for intervention of communication challenges. Communication challenges impede development of social skills... and the cycle continues. Without the teacher's helpful intervention, children with communication deficits often present challenging behaviors.

Example of Inappropriate Behavior in Autism

Annie is a three year old diagnosed with autism level two. She has been receiving services at home for the past year but her family and her education team feel she would benefit from a preschool experience to be among her same-age peers.

Annie has been attending preschool for a full month. During this time, she has exhibited some challenging behaviors ranging from kicking, hitting, throwing toys and exiting the classroom unattended. Her behavior is not vindictive; rather, she has a high energy level and uses a minimal amount of verbal communication. She is also extremely sensitive to the rising noise level of the classroom. As the noise level increases, her activity level increases. Her mother reports Annie's morning schedule and getting dressed are often a challenge. Her socks must be on a certain way to avoid "sock bumps," her shoes tied a certain way, and her shirts and underclothes must be free of tags.

This morning Annie ran into the classroom twirling her new dress for all of her friends. It was picture day, and she was so excited to be able to wear her new dress. The morning progressed well in the regular routine until Annie learned that they would not be going outside because the playground was muddy and everyone was dressed for picture day. Annie cried a bit. She enjoyed her outside play.

Later, knowing the daily schedule well, Annie cleaned up and was getting her lunch box out of her cubby. The teacher smiled, and told her, "Annie, you remember this is when we have lunch. Today is different. Today we are going to have our pictures taken and then come back to the room for lunch." Annie cried a bit. The teacher helped her put her lunch box back and told her she was hungry too, but they wouldn't be long.

When they arrived downstairs for pictures, they were told the photographer was running a bit late, and it would probably be another fifteen minutes before he'd be able to start on the class. So, the teacher had the children sit down in the adjacent classroom while she read a couple of stories. Annie sat, confused. On a few occasions during the stories, she stood, twisting her hair, anxiously watching the flash in the next room. The teacher brought her back to the circle. Annie could not sit still. She began lightly kicking the boy next to her. When he moved away, she scooted closer, and kicked harder. This continued until both of them were standing, the boy trying to move elsewhere and Annie following right behind. The teacher intervened and suggested that Annie sit on one side of her and the boy sit on the other.

The photographer was now ready for the class so the children moved into the room and sat on the floor, each waiting for her turn. Annie sat down and immediately began twisting her hair and rocking as she anxiously watched the photographer. At each flash of the camera she stopped quickly and covered her eyes. When her teacher let her know that the photographer was ready to take her picture Annie went forward reluctantly and sat in the chair. The photographer repeated, "Look here, look at me," as Annie continued to look anxiously around at all of the equipment behind him. Unable to otherwise get her attention, the photographer walked up to Annie, held her chin to put it in place for the picture, and Annie bit his hand.

Classroom Strategies to Assist Positive Guidance

Why This Behavior?

As indicated earlier, children misbehave to avoid something or because they want something. In the prior example, Annie's day was off schedule, so she began the day with a lot of anxiety. She needed that structure. Her anxiety increased when she watched the photographer manipulate all of the odd pieces of equipment which looked nothing like the camera her mother uses to take her picture. When the photographer touched her she did not know how to respond to the touch of someone she'd just met and didn't know how to properly direct her anxiety. Annie would have benefited from more advance notice of the changes in schedule as well as a simple explanation of the photographer's equipment and his job.

Understanding Temperaments

It is important that teachers try to understand children and their various temperaments and behaviors so they can help prevent behavior problems before they start. Young children with or without autism often have difficultly expressing what they are feeling and are just beginning to learn strategies to self-regulate their emotions. Research (Kaiser & Rasminsky, 1999) indicates that the ability to change challenging behaviors reaches a peak in the first three years of life. After that point, while it is possible, it becomes more difficult to change negative behavior patterns, and children are likely to continue and add to those negative behaviors through the years.

Too often a child will express concern over an issue, and the adult in charge will respond with something akin to "Oh, you're fine. You're okay." Obviously, if a child is exhibiting signs of distress, he is not fine. This is often the first sign that a child is trying to cope. If the teacher does not intervene, she will likely find herself challenged with a child's negative behavioral response. From the beginning, it is especially important that the teacher has conversations with the parent of the child with autism to learn about his/her specific challenges and to better understand what might trigger a challenging behavior.

Helping Children Understand Feelings

Children should understand that feelings are natural. Everyone has feelings. For instance, it's okay to be angry, but there are ways to express anger rather than hurt another person. Time should be spent giving children the words they need to express and understand feelings.

For instance, when a child approaches the teacher upset because someone has called her a name, the teacher can help her understand the reason she's upset by saying, "You're upset he called you a baby. You are not a baby. That hurt your feelings. Go tell him that he hurt your feelings." This way, the child not only learns the reason she is feeling sad, but can learn to independently put words to her feelings in her own defense.

The child with autism will especially need to learn words to understand feelings, or may not otherwise understand when he has upset someone, has upset himself, or even made another child happy. There are several stories listed in Appendix B which might help young children understand their emotions and address issues of self-regulation.

Feeling Safe

Feeling safe extends to the children's emotional well-being as well as physical safety. Children need to understand that we all have feelings, we all make mistakes and we do the wrong thing sometimes. They need to understand that we are all alike as much as we are all different and that every person belongs and is accepted. Every class-

room should have a set of rules to reinforce safety and to facilitate classroom management. The rules need to be simple and few in number. Three rules to consider, which cover all aspects of physical and social-emotional safety and classroom management, include:
- Be safe,
- Take care of yourself and your friends,
- Follow the directions.

An important step when developing classroom rules is to also pass the rules to families for reinforcement at home, and to other teachers and classrooms in the school with whom the children associate. Many children, especially children with autism, do NOT generalize skills. While they might follow these rules in your classroom, once they step out of the classroom, it is not something they will continue.

We're All Friends

Take care of yourself and your friends reinforces the view that everyone is welcome and everyone in the classroom is a friend. If a child hurts another, he should be responsible for taking care of the child. As adults, our first instinct is to make the child say, "I'm sorry." This is a mistake. Unless the child has done something horrific, he is probably not at all sorry he hurt someone. He is sorry he got caught! By directing the child to simply say "I'm sorry," the child is not really accepting responsibility for his actions. Rather, he is following your direction with little concern for the welfare of his victim. We do need to let the child know what he did was wrong, and why it was wrong. We should tell him, "We don't hit. Hitting hurts. You need to see if Sarah is okay" and follow this up with a strategy so that he needs to take responsibility for hurting someone. Children should learn that they will always be responsible for their actions.

Taking Responsibility for Challenging Behavior

To help children learn to take responsibility for challenging behavior, a strategy that works well is to have the child face the child he hurt, put one hand on his shoulder and ask him "Are you okay?" If the child answers she is not okay, then he should be directed to remain with the child until she indicates she is okay. He can also be directed to get her a tissue for her tears, ice if she needs it, or do anything else to assist the child he hurt. This technique puts the responsibility for making peace between the two children, rather than on the teacher. This strategy reinforces feeling "safe" in the classroom as the children develop an understanding that teachers and friends are all looking out for one another. This strategy also fosters independence by teaching how to take responsibility for actions, a life skill which will transfer to later years. After teaching, repeating and initially prompting the strategy, the children begin to initiate it on their own.

Since children with autism have deficits in understanding another's perspective and feelings, this strategy of being responsible for behavior goes a long way toward helping them to understand the consequences of exhibiting challenging behaviors. Again, most children, especially children with autism, do not generalize skills or carry over behaviors from one environment to the other. For this strategy to work successfully, it should be shared with families and with other classroom teachers with whom the children associate.

Managing Time and Guidance

As indicated in the section on environment, time is a difficult measure for young children, especially when they are waiting their turn. Sand timers help provide guidance to children when they are waiting for a turn to share a toy as in, "You may have a turn on the bike when Lisa is finished. Lisa is going to ride it for three minutes.

The sand will all be at the bottom of the timer when it is your turn." Then remind the other child, "Lisa, it will be Mikail's turn after this three minute timer is finished." If a timer is not available, the waiting children could be directed to sing a particular song, or the teacher can suggest that the children count to ten or twenty to determine when it is time to share. Another strategy for waiting to take turns is laminated stop/wait (red) and go/my turn (green) signs to help make turn-taking concrete.

Encouraging and Reinforcing Positive Behavior

Of course, one of the most important aspects of positive guidance is to recognize, encourage and reinforce positive behavior. To coin an old phrase, "Catch them at being good." When a child shares something, teachers should recognize the transfer, and let the child know. "Jason, I know you were really enjoying that truck. Thank you for passing it to Ryan for his turn." Also, reinforce to the

waiting child, "Ryan, thank you for waiting so patiently. Remember to thank Jason for sharing." And, when you can tell that a child is struggling with self-control, help him out before he loses control: "Mitchell, I see that you are so angry and that you are trying so hard to use your words. Beth, do you see how upset he is? He really worked hard on that tower, and you knocked it down. Mitchell, would you like Beth to help you rebuild it? Beth, see if he's okay…"

Thank you for taking the time to read this text. I hope that in doing so you have gained a little more understanding about educating young children with autism. As you share your teaching gift with the little ones, I hope you continue to enjoy the many kindnesses and riches you inspire in the heart of every child.

APPENDIX A

Preschool-age children function better with daily routines. Visual schedules support early literacy and sequencing skills while accommodating visual learners. Visual schedules help increase independence, assist with transitioning and inform children in advance of potential changes in the daily schedule.

These cards are best laminated, placed in order and attached to velcro so they can be moved around when schedules change, or taken down after each activity is completed during the day.

Similar pictures can be generated for choices of songs, games and other small and large group activities during the day.

Today's Schedule

Arrive at School

Story/Circle Time

Show and Tell

Bathrooom/ Hand Washing 	Craft 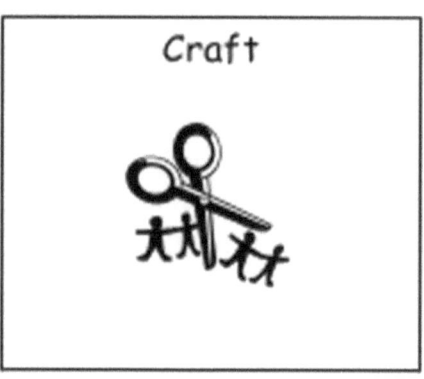
Lunch 	Classroom Play 
Cooking 	Music 

Appendix A

Outside Play

End of Day/ Going Home

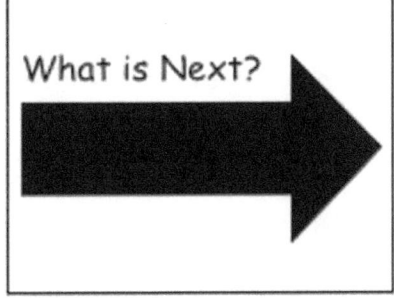

What is Next?

This arrow can be used to mark the current place in the schedule.

APPENDIX B

Picture books for young children which help develop social/emotional competence and explain autism:

Elmer (McKee, D., Lothrop, Lee & Shepard Books) — diversity, self-worth & acceptance

Glad Monster/Sad Monster (Emberly E., & Miranda A., Scholastic Books) — expressing feelings

Go Away Big Green Monster (Emberly E., Scholastic Books) — overcoming fear

I Like Me! (Carlson, N., Trumpet Club Books)— positive self-esteem

I'm Gonna Like Me (Curtis, J., Cornell, Harper Collins Books) — positive self-esteem

It's Not Easy Being a Bunny (Sadler, M. Random House Beginner Books) — positive self-esteem

It's Okay to be Different (Parr,T., Little Brown & Co.) — understanding differences

Just the Way You Are (Pfister, M. North-South Books) — self-worth & acceptance

Let's Be Enemies (Udry, J. & Sendak M., Harper Collins Publishers) — value of friendship & forgiving

Llama, Llama, Mad at Mama (Dewdney, A. Viking Books) — emotional self-regulation

Mama, If You Had A Wish (Modesitt, Spowart, Aladdin Paperbacks) — understanding we all make mistakes and sometimes do the wrong thing, but we're always loved

Mama Zooms (Cowen-Fletcher, J., Scholastic)—family diversity

Mean Soup (Everitt, B., Voyager Books)— emotional self-regulation

New Friends, True Friends, Stuck Like Glue Friends (Kroll, V. & Rosely R., William B Berdman's Publishing Co.)— value of friendship

On Monday When it Rained (Kachenmeister, C. & Berthiaume, T. Houghton Mifflin Co.) — understanding feelings in self & others

Sometimes I'm Bombaloo (Vail, R. Heyo., Y., Scholastic Press) — emotional regulation

The Land of Many Colors (Klamath Co. Preschool, Scholastic Books) — recognizing and accepting differences

The Feelings Book (Parr, T., Little Brown & Company) — understanding emotions

The Kissing Hand, (Penn, A., Scholastic Books)— separation anxiety

The Rainbow Fish (Pfister, M., North-South Books)— value of friendship & sharing

The Way I Feel (Cain, J., Parenting Press) — understanding Feelings

When Sophie Gets Angry (Bang, M., Scholastic Inc.) — emotional self-regulation)

Words Are Not for Hurting (Verdick, E. & Heinlen, M., Free Spirit Publishing) — understanding how words can be hurtful

Yo! Yes! (Raschka, C., Scholastic, Inc.) — making friends & importance of friendship

Picture books written especially for and about children with autism:

Friends Learn About Tobin (Murell, D., 2007, Future Horizons, Inc.) — value of friendship & understanding children with autism

I Have Autism: A Child's First Look at Autism (Crissey & Crissey, Super Duper Publications) — understanding autism

Tobin Learns to Make Friends (Murell, D., 2001, Future Horizons, Inc.) — learning how to play & get along with others

APPENDIX C

[Include pictures of the child so he also has visuals of what to do.]

HOW TO GREET SOMEONE

When I see someone I know, usually I try to smile and say "Hello." Sometimes they say "Hello" to me. Sometimes they might even stop to talk with me.

Sometimes I will shake their hand. Sometimes, when I am visiting a relative or a friend, I will try to give them a small hug.

Sometimes, if I am just passing someone I know, I can smile, I can wave, or I can just nod my head. Most people like it when I smile at them. Smiling can make people feel happy.

REFERENCES

Autism Society of America. (2010). *About autism.* Retrieved January 29, 2010, from http://www.autism-society.org.

Autism Society of America. (undated). *Building our future: Educating students on the autism spectrum.* Retrieved January 29, 2010, from http://www.autism-society.org.

Bee, H. & Boyd, D. (2007). *The developing child.* (11th ed.). NY: Person/Allyn & Bacon.

Bodrova, E., & Leong, D. J. (1996). *Tools of the mind: The Vygotskian approach to early childhood education.* Columbus Ohio: Merrill/Prentice Hall.

Bondy, A., & Frost, L. (2002). *A Picture's Worth: PECS and Other Visual Communication Strategies in Autism.* Bethesda, MD: Woodbine House.

Bredekamp, S., & Copple, C. (1997). *Developmentally appropriate practice in early childhood programs* (2nd ed.). Washington, DC: National Association for the Education of Young Children.

Bruey, C. (2004). *Demystifying autism spectrum disorders: A guide for parents and professionals.* Bethesda, MD: Woodbine House.

Center for Disease Control and Prevention. (2020). *Data and statistics on autism spectrum disorder.* Retrieved March 28, 2020 from CDC Website: https://www.cdc.gov/ncbddd/autism/data.html.

Circle of Inclusion. (2007). *Accommodating all children in the early childhood classroom.* Retrieved November 18, 2007, from http://www.circleofinclusion.org.

Circle of Inclusion. (2007). *Barriers to Inclusive Services.* Retrieved November 18, 2007, from http://www.circleofinclusion.org.

Copple, D. & Bredekamp, S. (2006). *Basics of developmentally appropriate practice: An introduction for teachers of children three to six.* Washington, DC: National Association for the Education of Young Children.

Council for Exceptional Children (CEC), Division for Early Childhood (DEC). (1999). *Position statement on interventions for challenging behavior.*

Young Exceptional Children (Monograph Series 1). Missoula, MT: CEC/DEC. Epstein, A. S. (2007). *The Intentional Teacher: Choosing the best strategies for young children's learning.* Washington, DC: National Association for the Education of Young Children.

Gray, C. (2000). *The new social story book.* Arlington, TX: Future Horizons, Inc.

Grandin, T. (1986/2005). *Emergence: Labeled autistic.* New York/Boston: Warner Books.

Hooper, S., Umansky, W. (2004). *Young children with special needs.* (4th ed.). Upper Saddle, NJ: Pearson/Merrill Prentice Hall.

Howley, M., & Arnold, E. (2005). *Revealing the hidden social code: Social stories for people with autistic spectrum disorders.* London: Jessica Kingsley Publishers.

Hull, K., Goldhaber, J. & Capone, A. (2002). *Opening doors: An introduction to inclusive early childhood education.* New York, NY: Houghton Mifflin Co.

Jensen, A. (2005). *When babies read: A practical guide to helping young children with hyperlexia, Asperger's syndrome and high-functioning autism.* Philadelphia, PA: Jessica Kingsley Publishers.

Jensen, E. (1998). *Teaching with the brain in mind.* Alexandria, VA: Association for Supervision and Curriculum Development.

Johnson, J., Christie, J. & Wardle, F. (2005). *Play, development and early education.* New York, NY: Pearson Education, Inc.

Kaiser, B. & Rasminsky, J. (1999). *Meeting the challenge: Effective strategies for challenging behaviors in early childhood environments.* Ontario, Canada: Canadian Child Care Federation.

Kluth, P. (2003). *"You're going to love this kid!" Teaching students with autism in the inclusive classroom.* Baltimore, MD: Brooks Publishing Co.

Koegel, R. L., & Koegel, L. K. (2006). *Pivotal response treatments for autism: communication, social and academic development.* Baltimore, MD: Paul H. Brookes Publishing Co.

Kutscher, M. (2005). *Kids in the syndrome mix of ADHD, LD, Asperger*s, Tourette's bipolar, and more!* Philadelphia, PA: Jessica Kingsley Publishers.

Landa, R., Holman, K.C. & Garret-Meyer, E. (2007). Social and communication development in toddlers with early and later diagnosis of autism spectrum disorders. *Archives of General Psychiatry, 64,* 853-664.

Lovaas, O.I., Schreibman, L., Koegel R.L. & Rehm, R. (1971). Selective responding by autistic children to multiple sensory input. *Journal of Abnormal Psychology, 77,* 211-222.

Mooney, C. (2000). *Theories of childhood.* St. Paul, MN: Red Leaf Press.

Nekovei, D. L., & Ermis, S. A. (2006). Creating classrooms that promote rich vocabularies for at-risk learners. *Young Children, 61(5),* 90-95.

Rao, S., & Gagie, B. (2006). Learning through seeing and doing: Visual supports for children with autism. *Teaching Exceptional Children, 4238(6),* 26-33.

Reading is Fundamental. (2007). *RIF's guide to reading aloud for your children.* Retrieved January 12, 2008 from www.rif.org.

Rocha, M., Schreibman, L., & Stahmer, A. (2007). Effectiveness of training parents to teach joint attention in children with autism. *Journal of Early Intervention, 29(2),* 154-172.

Snow, K. (2001). *Disability is natural: Revolutionary common sense for raising successful children with disabilities.* Woodland Park, CO: BraveHeart Press.

Soenksen, D., & Alper, S. (2006). Teaching a young child to appropriately gain attention of peers using a social story intervention. *Focus on Autism and Other Developmental Disabilities, 21(1),* 36-44.

Stillman, W. (2003). *Demystifying the autistic experience: A humanistic introduction for parents, caregivers and educators.* Philadelphia: PA: Jessica Kingsley Publishers.

U.S. Centers for Disease Control & Prevention (2007). *Autism information center:Prevalence.* Washington, DC. Retrieved November 6, 2007, from http://www.cdc.gov.

U.S. Department of Education (2004). *Building the legacy of the IDEA 2004.* Washington, DC. Retrieved October 19, 2007, from http://idea.ed.gov.

Volkmar, F. R., Paul, R., Klin, A., & Cohen, D. (2005). *Handbook of autism and pervasive developmental disorders: Assessment, interventions, and policy* (3 ed. Vol. 2). Hoboken, NJ: John Wiley & Sons, Inc.

Willis, C. (2006). *Teaching Young Children with Autism Spectrum Disorder.* Beltsville, MD: Gryphon House, Inc.

Wolfberg, P. (2003). *Peer play and the autism spectrum.* Shawnee Mission, KS: Autism Asperger Publishing Company.

Foreword References

Gartrell, D. (2004). *The power of guidance.* Washington, DC: National Association for the Education of Young Children.

Division for Early Childhood and National Association for the Education of Young Children. (2009). *Early childhood inclusion: A joint position statement of the Division for Early Childhood (DEC) and the National Association for the Education of Young Children.* Missoula, MT: DEC.

Organizations Specializing in Autism Research and Information

Autism Society
4340 East-West Highway
Suite 350
Bethesda, MD 20814
800-328-8476
www.autism-society.org

The ARC of the United States
1825 K Street, NW
Suite 1200
Washington, DC 20006
800-433-5255
www.thearc.org

Autism Science Foundation
106 W. 32nd Street, Suite 182
New York, NY 10003
914-810-9100
www.autismsciencefoundation.org

Autism Speaks (NY OFFICE)
1 East 33rd Street, 4th Floor
New York, NY 10016
646-385-8500

Kennedy Krieger Institute
Center for Autism and Related Disabilities
3901 Greenspring Avenue
Baltimore, MD 21211
800-873-3377
www.kennedykrieger.org

U.S. Centers for Disease Control and Prevention
Autism Information Center, Washington, DC.
http://www.cdc.gov

SUGGESTIONS FOR FURTHER READING

(These publications are NOT included in the following annotated bibliography, but are the author's suggestions for further reading.)

Bruey, C. (2004). *Demystifying autism spectrum disorders: A guide for parents and professionals.* Bethesda, MD: Woodbine House.
— For those most interested in learning more about autism, this book is a wonderful overview of autism spectrum disorders in easy to understand language.

Grandin, T. (1986). *Emergence: Labeled autistic.* New York/Boston: Warner Books.
— Dr. Grandin as a very successful adult with Aspergers Syndrome. In this book, she reflects on her childhood memories, the challenges autism presented in her life, and lessons learned.

Gray, C. (2000). *The new social story book.* Arlington, TX: Future Horizons, Inc.
— This book is a wonderful guide to writing social stories for young children with autism.

Kaiser, B. & Rasminsky, J. (1999). *Meeting the challenge: Effective strategies for challenging behaviors in early childhood environments.* Ontario, Canada: Canadian Child Care Federation.
— An easy-to-read book outlining positive guidance for all young children.

Smith, M. (2001). *Teaching play skills to children with autistic spectrum disorder.* New York: DRL Books.
— A guide on the importance of play which includes games and activities to play with children on the autism spectrum.

Stillman, W. (2005). *The everything parent's guide to children with Aspergers syndrome: Help, hope, and guidance.* Avon, MA: Adams Media/F&W Publishing Co.
— Easy to read text with strategies for guidance, and information on Aspergers.

Warner, L., Lynch, S., Nabors, D., & Simpson, C. (2007). *Inclusive lesson plans throughout the year*. Beltsville, MD: Gryphon House, Inc.
— A handbook of lesson plans outlining ways to include children with all abilities and physical or mental challenges in the mainstream classroom.

Willis, C. (2006). *Teaching Young Children with Autism Spectrum Disorder.* Beltsville, MD: Gryphon House.
— An excellent manual devoted to teaching strategies for children with autism (but may be geared for a less fully-inclusive environment). Guided activities and instructions in learning domains.

Wolfberg, P. (2003). *Peer play and the autism spectrum*. Shawnee Mission, KS: Autism Asperger Publishing Company.
— A program developed to help children with autism learn to play through interaction with their peers. Guided activities and instructions.

Annotated Bibliography

Baker, J. (2001). *The social skills picture book: Teaching play, emotion and communication to children with autism.* Arlington, TX: Future Horizons, Inc.
— Information on the benefits of using picture books and social stories for children with autism.

Bee, H., Boyd, D. (2007). *The developing child* (11 ed.). Pearson Education.
— Psychology text book which outlines the developmental life of the child.

Bodrova, E., & Leong, D. J. (1996). *Tools of the mind: The Vygotskian approach to early childhood education.* Columbus Ohio: Merrill/Prentice Hall.
— Book outlining Vygotskian approach and theories, and ways to apply the theories to classroom strategies.

Bondy, A., & Frost, L. (2002). *A Picture's Worth: PECS and other visual communication strategies in autism.* Bethesda, MD: Woodbine House.
— Information on benefits of using PECS.

Bredekamp, S., & Copple, C. (1997). *Developmentally appropriate practice in early childhood programs* (2 ed.). Washington, DC: National Association for the Education of Young Children.
— Information on appropriate developmental practice in all domains for all early childhood educators, as well as practical application for the classroom.

Charman, T., & Stone, W. (2006). *Social & communication development in autism spectrum disorders: Early identification, diagnosis & intervention.* New York, NY: The Guilford Press.
— Quite technical although a thorough text outlining deficits and strategies for social & communication development in autism.

Chenfeld, M. B. (2006). Wanna play? *Young Children, 61(6),* 34-42.
— Short article on importance of play.

Circle of Inclusion. (2007). *Accommodating all children in the early childhood classroom.* Retrieved November 18, 2007, from http://www.circleofinclusion.org.
— Organization dedicated to inclusionary practices for all children.

Early Childhood Funders. (2007). *Play in the early years: Key to school success.*
— Policy Brief, Bay Area Early Childhood Funders. Retrieved November 30, 2007 from www.4children.org/ecf.htm. Brief on the importance of play in childhood development and cognition.

Epstein, A. S. (2007). *The Intentional Teacher: Choosing the best strategies for young children's learning.* Washington, DC: National Association for the Education of Young Children.
— An excellent source of information on all aspects of an exemplary preschool program.

Etscheidt, S. (2006). Least restrictive and natural environments for young children with disabilities. *Topics in Early Childhood Special Education, 26(3),* 167-178.
— Overview/Papers written on inclusion issues. Includes information for general education preschool directors considering including children with disabilities.

Flowers, T. (2000). *The color of autism: Methods to reach and educate children on the autism spectrum.* Arlington, TX: Future Horizons, Inc.
— Easy-to-read book written by an autism teacher on strategies to use for teaching children with autism.

Gartrell, D. (2004). *The power of guidance: Teaching social-emotional skills in early childhood classrooms.* Clifton Park, NY: Thomson/Delmar Learning.
— Excellent resource on positive guidance for young children.

Grandin, T. (1995). *Thinking in pictures and other reports from my life with autism*. New York, NY: Vintage Books.
— Also the author of *Emergence: Labelled Autistic*. Dr. Grandin, a successful adult with Asperger's Syndrome shares the various ways she learned by developing series of pictures and icons, and lessons learned.

Greenspan, S. I., & Weider, S. (2006). *Engaging autism: Using the floortime approach to help children relate, communicate and think* (Vol. 1). Cambridge, MA: Da Capo Press.
— Author of *The Floortime Approach*, Greenspan modifies his approach with strategies to teach young children with autism.

Hooper, S. R., & Umansky, W. (2004). *Young children with special needs* (4th ed.). Upper Saddle River, NJ: Pearson Merrill Prentice Hall.
— Text book which includes detailed information on early childhood development, theories, and approaches to educating young children with disabilities.

Howley, M., & Arnold, E. (2005). *Revealing the hidden social code: Social stories for people with autistic spectrum disorders*. London: Jessica Kingsley Publishers.
— A manual explaining the key elements of social stories for ASDs.

Jensen, E. (1998). *Teaching with the brain in mind*. Alexandria, VA: Association for Supervision and Curriculum Development.
— Easy to read book on how the human brain learns along with strategies for teaching based on the information.

Kennedy Krieger Institute. (2007). *Autism spectrum disorders (ASD) and pervasive development disorders (PDD)*. Retrieved September 15, 2007, from kennedykrieger.org.
— KKI runs an excellent on-line reference center for the general public and families on the most current information on ASDs.

Killoran, I. & Brown, M., (2006). *There's room for everyone. Accommodations supports, and transition infancy to postsecondary*. Olney, MD: Association for Childhood Education International.

Kluth, P. (2003). *"You're going to love this kid!" Teaching students with autism in the inclusive classroom.* Baltimore, MD: Brooks Publishing Co.

— An excellent publication on inclusionary benefits and strategies throughout the school years.

Kluth, P. (2003). *"You're going to love this kid!" Teaching students with autism in the inclusive classroom.* Baltimore, MD: Brooks Publishing Co.

— A wonderful book of strategies for including children with autism in elementary and secondary schools. From this book comes the well-known phrase, "If you know one person with autism, you know one person with autism."

Koegel, R. L., & Koegel, L. K. (2006). *Pivotal response treatments for autism: Communication, social and academic development.* Baltimore, MD: Paul H. Brookes Publishing Co.

— Text outlining pivotal response training for autism.

Kutscher, M. (2005). *Kids in the syndrome mix of ADHD, LD, Asperger's, tourette's bipolar, and more!* Philadelphia, PA: Jessica Kingsley Publishers.

— Information provided by a doctor of neurology on many of the dual diagnoses associated with ASDs.

Mooney, C. (200). *Theories of childhood.* St. Paul, MN: Red Leaf Press.

— Outlines many of best recognized theories of childhood, including Dewey, Erikson, Montessori, Piaget and Vygotsky.

Murdock, L., Cost, H., & Tieso, C. (2007). Measurement of social communication skills of children with autism spectrum disorders during interactions with typical peers. *Focus on Autism and Other Developmental Disabilities, 22(3),* 160-171.

— Report on a study conducted to measure communication differences in children with autism when interacting with peers.

National Association for the Education of Young Children. (2007). *Early years are learning years: Choosing a preschool.* Retrieved November 25, 2007 from http://www.naeyc.org.

— NAEYC is the premier expert organization on early childhood education and development and their Website and articles therein reflect the wealth of their knowledge.

Preis, J. (2006). The effect of picture communication symbols on the verbal comprehension of commands by young children with autism. *Focus on Autism and Other Developmental Disabilities, 21(4),* 194-210.
— Study conducted to test the effectiveness of PECs in helping non-communicative children with autism.

Purcell, M. L., Horn, E., & Palmer, S. (2007). A qualitative study of the initiation and continuation of preschool inclusion programs. *Exceptional Children, 74(1),* 85-99.
— A study conducted on preschool inclusion programs which concluded there are too few pure inclusionary preschool practices in the US education system.

Quill, K. A. (1995). *Teaching children with autism: Strategies to enhance communication and socialization.* New York, NY: Delmar Publishers, Inc.
— More of a "technical" text outlining teaching strategies for teaching children with autism.

Rao, S., & Gagie, B. (2006). Learning through seeing and doing: Visual supports for children with autism. *Teaching Exceptional Children, 38(6),* 26-33.
— Article on importance of visual supports for children with autism.

Reading is Fundamental. (2007). *RIF's guide to reading aloud for your children.* Retrieved January 12, 2008 from www.rif.org.
— RIF provides on-line reference center with the most current information on reading and literacy.

Reynhout, G., & Carer, M. (2007). Social story efficacy with a child with autism spectrum disorder and moderate intellectual disability. *Focus on Autism and Other Developmental Disabilities, 22(3),* 171-182.
— Research on the benefits of social story intervention for children with autism.

Rocha, M., Schreibman, L., & Stahmer, A. (2007). Effectiveness of training parents to teach joint attention in children with autism. *Journal of Early Intervention, 29(2),* 154-172.
— Article on importance of promoting joint attention at the

earliest age and getting parents involved in joint attention training.

Seitz, H. (2006). The plan: Building on children's Interests. *Young Children, 61(2),* 36-41.

— Article outlining the importance of choosing classroom activities based on children's interest.

Snow, K. (2001). *Disability is natural: Revolutionary common sense for raising successful children with disabilities.* Woodland Park, CO: BraveHeart Press.

— A must read for parents of children with disabilities! Fun, comforting text helps families realize how important each individual person is to our world community.

Stanton-Chapman, T., Kaiser, A., & WolAnnery, M. (2006). Building social communication skills in Head Start children using storybooks: The effects of prompting on social interactions. *Journal of Early Intervention, 28(3),* 197-212.

— Study conducted on children in the Head Start program using social storybooks to increase social skills.

Stillman, W. (2003). *Demystifying the autistic experience: A humanistic introduction for parents, caregivers and educators.* Philadelphia: PA: Jessica Kingsley Publishers.

— William Stillman is a very successful adult with Asperger's Syndrome who shares his experiences and experiences of his peers with autism. Stillman is a wonderful public speaker on autism as well.

U.S. Department of Education (2004). *Building the legacy of the IDEA 2004.* Washington, DC. Retrieved October 19, 2007, from http://idea.ed.gov.

— Government source for specific information on the Individuals with Disabilities Act.

U.S. Department of Education (2005). Center on high quality personnel in inclusive preschool settings. *Federal Register, 70(237),* 73456-73459.

— DOE article on the importance of hiring highly educated personnel to teach at the preschool level.

Volkmar, F. R., Paul, R., Klin, A., & Cohen, D. (2005). *Handbook of autism and pervasive developmental disorders: diagnosis, development, neurobiology, and behavior* (3 ed. Vol. 1). Hoboken, NJ: John Wiley & Sons, Inc.
-AND-
Volkmar, F. R., Paul, R., Klin, A., & Cohen, D. (2005). *Handbook of autism and pervasive developmental disorders: Assessment, interventions, and policy* (3 ed. Vol. 2). Hoboken, NJ: John Wiley & Sons, Inc.
— Two very technical handbooks on everything known about autism by the year 2005.

About the Author

KAREN GRIFFIN ROBERTS holds a Bachelor of Individualized Study (BIS) in Early Childhood Development: A Study in Autism, from George Mason University. In 2007 she completed a summer intern program at the Johns Hopkins Kennedy Krieger Institute's Center for Autism and Related Disorders, Baltimore, Maryland, under the direction of Dr. Katherine Holman. In 2010, she received her Masters Degree in Education with an Endorsement in Early Childhood Special Education from George Mason University.

Ms. Roberts has raised an adult son with autism and has taught general preschool education for nineteen years.

In addition to teaching she has at times assumed Preschool Administrator, Education Coordinator and Teacher Supervision responsibilities. In 1998 she was honored with the Children's World, Northern Virginia District Area, Master Educator Award. In 1999, she received the Children's World Honor Teacher Award and was one of eighteen honorees chosen nationwide to attend the National Association for the Education of Young Children's 1999 annual conference.

In 2010, Ms. Roberts joined Virginia's Prince William County's Special Education team. She taught preschool students for seven years and for two years she taught kindergarten to grade two students with autism. She retired from teaching in 2019.

Her undergraduate project to develop a manual for preschool teachers to use for including children with autism in the classroom won George Mason University's BIS award for "Most Creative Project," May 16, 2009. Worldwide response to this project from preschool administrators, special education and general education preschool teachers and families has resulted in the publication of the first edition of this book, *Embracing Autism in Preschool: Successful Strategies for General Education Teachers*.

Ms. Roberts is also the author of the Let's Talk series of books for preschool parents and teachers. The idea for the series was drawn from the many questions special education families ask about their child's challenges in early development. The first of the series, *Let's Talk About Early Language Development* is co-authored with Ana G. Hoover (2013). The second in the series, *Let's Talk About Autism in Early Childhood* is authored by Ms. Roberts (2014). The final and third in the series, *Let's Talk About Early Childhood Social-Emotional Development* is co-authored by Ms. Hoover and Ms. Roberts (2020).

www.ingramcontent.com/pod-product-compliance
Lightning Source LLC
Chambersburg PA
CBHW021118080526
44587CB00010B/562